VERDI BARITONE : STUDIES IN TH

D0436723

T H E

VERDI

BARITONE

T H E

VERDI

BARITONE

STUDIES IN THE

DEVELOPMENT OF

DRAMATIC CHARACTER

Geoffrey Edwards and Ryan Edwards

INDIANA UNIVERSITY PRESS

BLOOMINGTON AND INDIANAPOLIS

The paper used in this publication meets the minimum requirements of American National Standard for Information Sciences—Permanence of Paper for Printed Library Materials, ANSI Z39.48-1984.

Manufactured in the United States of America

Library of Congress Cataloging-in-Publication Data
Edwards, Geoffrey, date

The Verdi baritone : studies in the development of dramatic character / Geoffrey Edwards and Ryan Edwards.
    p. cm.
Includes bibliographical references (p.   ).
ISBN 0-253-31949-8
    1. Verdi, Giuseppe, 1813-1901. Operas. 2. Verdi, Giuseppe, 1813-1901—Dramaturgy. I. Edwards, Ryan. II. Title.
ML410.V4E3   1994
782.1'092—dc20   93-27721
        1 2 3 4 5 99 98 97 96 95 94

Dedicated with love to

Leila Edwards

CONTENTS

Appendix: Plot Synopses

Acknowledgments

The authors gratefully acknowledge the many friends and colleagues who encouraged the development of this book and who generously shared their scholarly insights and rich performance experience in commenting on the manuscript. In particular, thanks to Dr. Richard Alderson, Dr. Albert Cirillo, Dr. Douglas Cole, Maestro Anton Coppola, Mr. Richard Covello, Mme Phyllis Curtin, Dr. Walter Ducloux, Maestro Peter Erös, Mr. Andrew Foldi, Mr. Malcolm Fraser, Mr. Robert Gay, Mr. Boris Goldovsky, Mr. Irving Guttman, Mme Lorna Haywood, Mr. Jerome Hines, Mr. Désiré Ligeti, Mr. Cornell MacNeil, the late Maestro Richard Marzollo, Mr. Dominic Missimi, Dr. Arthur Schoep, Mr. James Schwabacher, Mr. George Shirley, Maestro Alfredo Silipigni, Mr. Richard Torigi, Mr. Giorgio Tozzi, and Dr. Gideon Waldrop.

Special thanks also to Mme Francine Delacroix, Curator at the Bibliothèque Historique de la Ville de Paris; Professor Franco Rossi, Curator of the Archives of La Fenice; Professor Gianpiero Tintori, Director of the Museo Teatrale alla Scala; Professor Martin Chusid, Director of the American Institute for Verdi Studies; and the staff of the Northwestern University Interlibrary Loan Department for their assistance in the researching of this book.

Research for this book at European libraries and archives was funded in part by a generous grant from Northwestern University.

Verdi's Otello and Simon Boccanegra (revised version) in Letters and Documents (1988), edited and translated by Hans Busch, is cited by permission of Oxford University Press.

THE

VERDI

BARITONE

Introduction

By the late 1820s, Paris had become the focal point for the Romantic movement that was sweeping Europe, propelling both theatre and opera into a fresh exploration of dramaturgy and characterization. In 1827, the great English actor Charles Kemble came to Paris to star in a season of Shakespeare plays; these productions reintroduced continental Europe to the potential of a drama based on the dynamics of character psychology, rather than on the artificiality of neoclassical decorum.

The same year, Victor Hugo published his great manifesto of romanticism, the preface to *Cromwell*. Reacting to what he perceived as a lack of recognizable humanity in the characters of French neoclassical theatre, Hugo championed a Shakespearean model of characterization based on the interaction of antitheses—replacing theatrical types with striking individuals, incorporating the sublime and the grotesque into complex but unified portrayals.[1] By 1829, Alfred de Vigny's French translation of *Othello* appeared on stage, and Gioacchino Rossini produced perhaps his greatest psychological music-drama, *Guillaume Tell*, for the Paris Opéra. In 1830, the spirit of romanticism shook the theatrical establishment to its foundations with the tumultuous *succès du scandale* of Hugo's *Hernani* at the Comédie-Française. A new dramatic era had dawned.

In the following decade, Italian composers, including Gaetano Donizetti, Vincenzo Bellini, and Saverio Mercadante, adopted the dynamics of Romantic characterization in their operas. The Metastasian formula, which relied on a schematic juxtaposition of contrasting emotional scenes to create a composite character portrait, yielded to the new Romantic emphasis on an organic approach to characterization. The simple counterpoising of psychologically static scenes was replaced by an exploration of the complex nexus of feelings and responses motivating the character moment by moment throughout the opera; the humanity of recognizable individuals was illuminated by a subtle interplay of words and music. Incisively delineated portrayals ranging from Lucrezia Borgia to Norma quickly emerged as masterpieces of *dramma per musica*, but such psychological dramaturgy was rarely applied to opera's baritone characters.

Throughout the *bel canto* period, the generic term *basso* usually suffices to designate either baritone or bass. The baritone's vocal range generally rests comfortably in the middle of his voice, with the visceral top register reserved for brilliant interpolations in the final moments of set pieces. Baritone characters are habitually older men weighted with an implacable authority drawn from family tradition, political power, social status, or religious prerogative. Usually providing the obligatory opposition to the love of the sopranos and tenors, baritone characters are largely confined to supporting roles, helping to illuminate the protagonists without achieving any real psychological complexity themselves. There is little evidence of subtextual development, little acknowledgment of an inner self beneath the public mask. Instead, baritone characters are relegated to a predictable array of stock scenes with primary emphasis on hectoring rage and belated remorse.[2] They are defined by the necessities of the opera plot, rather than emerging as dynamic individuals in their own right.

With Giuseppe Verdi, however, the baritone gains a dramatic ascendence not seen since the operas of Mozart. Like Shakespeare, the composer's favorite dramatist, Verdi was an indefatigable innovator who constantly explored new musicodramatic possibilities; one of his greatest contributions to operatic characterization was his transformation of the operatic baritone. Verdi used the unique potential of the baritone voice to create a gallery of subtly nuanced characters that are among the most complex and challenging in the operatic repertory.* He raised the baritone's vocal *tessitura*, clearly differentiating it from the bass and incorporating the top fifth of

---

* Even without exploring Verdi's comedic conception of the baritone in *Un Giorno di Regno* and *Falstaff*, the number of characters discussed here might easily have been doubled or even trebled. In considering the dramatic development of the Verdi baritone, however, the present study aims to be representative rather than exhaustive, suggesting the scope of Verdi's artistic vision throughout his career from the early triumph of *Nabucco* (1842) to the final glory of *Otello* (1887).

the voice as part of the baritone's normal range.³ The Verdi baritone must possess a voice powerful enough to rise over the most declamatory orchestration, but he must also exhibit dynamic flexibility and a spectrum of vocal colors capable of capturing the varied shadings of the human mind and heart. In the development of his baritone roles, Verdi tellingly explores the psychological tensions, ambiguous responses, and conflicting motivations that define each character's inner self. He reveals the human beings beneath the public masks in all their glory and ignominy, triumph and torment, hope and delusion. The Verdi baritone becomes the voice of humanity itself.⁴

Unfortunately, scholarly criticism often loses sight of the central importance of characterization in Verdi's operas, offering lengthy exegeses on specialized aspects of text, music, or staging without really exploring the dramatic interrelationship among these elements.⁵ In contrast to theatrical scholarship, much operatic criticism simply ignores the portrayal of character altogether in favor of bio-historical surveys, plot synopses, or musicological explications of form and structure.⁶ Most recently, another trend has emerged, one that attempts to contain the Italian operatic experience within the parameters of universalized theoretical paradigms drawn from pseudo-Wagnerian symbolism, feminism, Marxism, New Historicism, or a host of other currently fashionable approaches.⁷ Although each of these perspectives offers some valuable interpretations, neither microcosmic dissection nor macrocosmic schematization can fully elucidate Verdi's dramatic development of character, in which individual portrayals evolve organically from the interaction of text, music, and staging.⁸

Marginalized in scholarship, the complexity of Verdi's baritone characters is also frequently obfuscated in performance by the conceits of current concept stagings that claim to make opera more "relevant" to modern audiences. The conventions of the lyric stage require the audience to accept a greater degree of metatheatricality in opera than in spoken theatre.[9] In the magnitude of its dramatic conflicts, in the depth of emotion it elicits, in the expansiveness of its stage presentation, and above all in the elevation of its lyrical expression, opera aggrandizes daily reality. Yet, at its best, opera serves as an enlarging mirror that both reflects and heightens the reality of human life. The coexistence of theatricality and recognizable realism in opera was an accepted part of operatic characterization in the nineteenth century;[10] in the view of many modern producers and directors, however, this integration of styles threatens to undermine opera's dramatic viability. As a result, the components of nineteenth-century performance are often dichotomized, with metatheatricality being suppressed in favor of realistic illusion, or realism being abandoned in an appropriation of the presentational techniques of twentieth-century theatre.

Rigoletto is a case in point, for frequent revivals have generated a seemingly insatiable demand for fresh insights and novel approaches: the lavish historicism of Margarita Wallmann (Strasbourg, 1980) or Jean-Pierre Ponnelle (San Francisco, 1981); the modern-dress versions of Jonathan Miller (London, 1982) and August Everding (Cologne, 1987); or the symbolism of Harry Kupfer (Berlin, 1983) and Hans Neuenfels (Berlin, 1986). The dramatic complexity of the opera certainly sustains a variety of interpretive perspectives. In terms of characterization, however, many concept productions are less than satisfying because of their inability to maintain the balance of theatrical grandeur and recognizable humanity in the characters.

Neuenfels' staging of *Rigoletto* for the Deutsche Oper Berlin (1986)[11] turns the complex individuals of the opera into symbolic puppets, subverting their potential to appeal not only to the mind but also to the heart. For the abduction of Gilda, Neuenfels places Rigoletto's daughter in a glass box; the courtiers line up across the back of a bare stage, while Rigoletto helps Marullo and Ceprano carry a gigantic key. This staging certainly provides a pointed caption for Rigoletto's complicity in the loss of his treasure, and it also comments on the role of women as mere possessions in a male-dominated society. But as Rigoletto's almost inarticulate anguish at the end of the act testifies, Gilda is far more than an objectified possession.

Miller's "Little Italy" production for the English National Opera (1982),[12] on the other hand, undercuts the theatrical grandeur of the opera, trying to make the story of *Rigoletto* more accessible by setting the piece in modern surroundings and dress. Contemporary trappings, however, do not necessarily heighten the "relevance" of an opera for a modern audience: does the audience really identify more with a singing hunchbacked bartender than with a singing hunchbacked jester? Draped in motley or in white linen, Rigoletto is, at least superficially, outside the bounds of real life.

Ultimately, the enduring dramatic appeal of Verdi's baritone characters springs not from their outer trappings but from their inner selves. They are not just larger than life; they are both "grand et vrai" (great and true).[13] In their superficial historical context, in the particulars of their elevated tales, these characters are far removed from ordinary life in either the nineteenth century or today. But whether in the guise of jester, king, ensign, or bourgeois, the Verdi baritone embodies a quintessential humanity, expressing needs and temptations, confusions and understandings, griefs and joys that transcend the particulars of time and place. The Verdi baritone becomes a pilgrim on a voyage of self-discovery, and in the course of his journey he provides scholar, performer, and audience alike with greater insight into the essence of personal identity, into the suffering and delight of existence, into the struggle of the individual in a universe that is often beyond control and even comprehension, into the values that give meaning to human life.

Nabucco

Biblical spectacle, the crown jewel of early nineteenth-century French costume drama, seems an incongruous vehicle for intimate psychological character study, and yet it is in the setting of such an unlikely subject as *Nabucodonosor* (1842) that the dramatic potential of the Verdi baritone is first manifested. As Shakespeare's early history plays foreshadow the subtler and more profound vision of the great tragedies, so the character of Nabucodonosor, or Nabucco, as he is called in the opera, adumbrates the later dramatic portraits in which Verdi's exploration of personal identity and humanity's place in a larger order of existence reach consummate expression.

Contemporary critics were enthralled by *Nabucco*, the reviewer for the *Illustrated London News* declaring, "The more we hear this opera, the more convinced we are that Verdi's genius has here reached the highest point to which it can attain. The splendid harmonies and dramatic effects, and the no less varied and delightful melodies with which this opera abounds, entitles it to a place among the works of the greatest masters."[1] Yet, in retrospect Verdi himself was less satisfied, declaring in a letter to Antonio Somma a decade after the première that he would now refuse to set another subject in the genre of *Nabucco*.[2]

Verdi underscores with particular insight the essential limitations of an opera drawn from the tradition of historical spectacle: subordination of character to the implacable demands of theatrical effect and plot convolution.[3] Although later in his career Verdi would take an active role in shaping his own libretti, as a young composer he accepted Temistocle Solera's text for *Nabucco* virtually unchanged and confined his musical characterizations within the epic structure of the libretto.[4] As the *Gazzetta Musicale di Milano* noted with ironic praise, "Inoltre il soggetto biblico, ricco di grandiosità teatrale e di scenica poesia, si presta a dovere all'ampiezza delle nostre maggiori scene. Il signor Verdi mostrò di aver saputo ben comprendere le idee del Solera, e audacemente sicuro di sè adoperò a interpretare i suoi drammatici concetti." (In addition, the biblical subject, rich in theatrical grandeur and picturesque poetry, lends itself to the demands of our great stages. Signor Verdi showed he well understood Solera's ideas and, audaciously sure of himself, set about interpreting his dramatic concepts.)[5] Thus, while Verdi's musical characterization frequently imbues Nabucco with a resonance and complexity that transcend the libretto, the parameters imposed by the text are often intractable.

The French source play for the opera, *Nabuchodonosor* (1836) by Anicet-Bourgeois and Francis Cornu, is a monumental display piece, in which the primacy of stunning *coups de théâtre*, striking tableaux, and breathtaking decor makes subtlety of characterization irrelevant, if not impossible. Solera's libretto, in turn, hews closely to this source, condensing and conflating, but retaining the original dramatic structure and character delineations.[6] As in the play, Nabucco himself appears only in several climactic crisis scenes, a dramaturgical technique that mitigates against nuanced psychological exploration and mandates episodic and often diffused character development.

A charged atmosphere of ominous anticipation is created in the opening scenes of the opera as the terrified Hebrews await the arrival of Nabucco and his conquering troops at the temple of Solomon. Heralded as an imperious subjugator, Nabucco fittingly mounts the steps of the temple on horseback; this visual image is quickly subverted, however, by both the banal pomposity of the *banda*, which engulfs the king's arrival in a frenzy of triviality, and the anticlimactic nonchalance of Nabucco's first words. Anicet-Bourgeois' Nabuchodonosor declaims with suitable bombast, "Oui, gloire à Nabuchodonosor!.. c'est le vainqueur et le maître du peuple de Dieu" (Yes, glory to Nabuchodonosor! the conqueror and master of the people of God);[7] Nabucco, in contrast, musters only an enervated "Di Dio che parli?" (What are you saying of God?).[8]

The very nature of the dramatic situation in Solera's libretto further highlights a sense of hollowness in Nabucco's royal power. While Anicet-Bourgeois' protagonist enters the temple on his own terms, granting freedom to Ismaël as a favor to Phénenna, Solera's Nabucco is helpless because his daughter is held hostage by Zaccaria. As he growls to himself,

Nabucco's words are those of impotent fury: "Tremin, gl'insani del mio, del mio furore" (60; Let the madmen tremble at my fury). Verdi suggests the suppression of the king's volcanic potential with a *sotto voce andante* in which jagged dotted rhythms and propulsive triplets burst through the self-consciously restrained B on "Tremin" as does the ominous blast of a horn reverberating above the muted murmurs of strings in the orchestration.

As Nabucco vows that all Zion will drown in a sea of blood, his vocal line takes on a pattern of explosion and suppression, leaping a sixth to D-sharp only to fall again to F-sharp on "In mar,.. in mar di sangue" and "fra pianti, fra pianti e lai" (60; in a sea of blood, with tears and laments). Yet, the *bel canto* lyricism in these phrases subverts the sanguinary fury of the text. There is a greater depth of humanity in Nabucco than his public display of brutal authority will admit; as his vocal line swells to top E before an almost caressing denouement on "l'empia Sionne scorrer dovrà" (60-61; wicked Zion must drown), it is as if Nabucco were unconsciously revealing a glimpse of the inner man concealed behind his arrogant mask.

Verdi completes this dramatic subversion of kingly preten-
sions by quickly confining Nabucco within a static ensemble.
The invincible conqueror is reduced to repeating *sotto voce*
threats throughout a prolonged standoff as Fenena pleads for
mercy, Abigaille hopes for the death of her rival, and the
assembled Hebrews offer prayers to God. The limitations of
his royal power are clear, and his hubris thus stands out in
even sharper relief when Nabucco declares, "Ben l'ho chiamato
in guerra, ma venne il vostro Dio? Tema ha di me: resistermi,
stolti, chi mai, chi mai potrà?" (79; I called your God to battle,
but did He come? He fears me: fools, who can resist me?).

Ironically, Ismaele, not Nabucco, finally saves Fenena,
though the king immediately announces the execution of his
own terrible revenge: "Mio furor, non più costretto, fa dei vinti
atroce scempio" (81; My fury, no longer constrained, will
make terrible slaughter of the vanquished). Nabucco's *gioja
feroce* is clear in the trumpeting vocal line and whirlwind
orchestration of this Donizettian *stretta*, yet the king is quickly
submerged in the maelstrom he has loosed, his individual
identity lost in the massed cries of vengeance and lamentation
that bring the act to a close.

The real source of Nabucco's strength as both a ruler and a
man lies not in egotism and hatred but in love; and in the second act Nabucco gains new power and majesty through his
selfless defense of Fenena. Again, the king's entrance becomes
a *coup de théâtre*, coming in the final moments of the act as
Abigaille tries to seize the regent's crown from Fenena. The
parallels with the dramatic structure of the first act are clear,
but in contrast to the hollowness of "Di Dio che parli,"
Nabucco finds a new voice as he seizes the crown from
Abigaille and places it on his own head, turning his royal

power into a bulwark of defense to protect his child.[9] This act of self-abnegation and love imbues Nabucco with real strength, and, for the first time in the opera, the ringing declamation of the Verdi baritone's top register is heard, the vocal line rising to a *fortissimo* sustained top F underscored with driving orchestration for the challenge, "Dal capo mio la prendi!" (139; Take it from my head!).

This compelling moment of music-drama is quickly obscured, however, by the conventionalities of the ensuing ensemble. The jagged leaps in Nabucco's *andantino* vocal line, marked *sotto voce e cupo* and underscored with the suspended menace of *piano* strings and woodwinds, are well suited to the king's "S'appressan gl'istanti d'un'ira fatale" (140; The moments of fatal wrath approach). But as this melody is taken up in turn by principals and chorus, individual musical characterization inevitably gives way to a generalized emotional patina.

Faced with the betrayal of his friends and the defiance of his foes, Nabucco tries to reassert his own sense of kingship. He denounces the treacherous Babylonians, their priests, and the god that led them to betray their king; he reviles the defeated but intractable Hebrews and their God; he even turns, at last, on his beloved Fenena when she declares that she will die with the condemned Hebrews. Confronted by ubiquitous denial of the royal power that has heretofore defined his self-identity, Nabucco struggles to stave off personal annihilation with an overreaching grasp at the power of Heaven. In his alienation and frustration, he finally cries out with disastrous hubris, "Giù! pròstrati!.. non son più re, son Dio" (155; Down! Prostrate yourself! I am no longer king, I am God). Nabucco denies his very humanity, placing himself outside the realm of mortal men and abjuring the paternal love that was the source of his inner strength just moments before.

Drained of the indomitable power of love that infused his defense of Fenena, Nabucco's arrogation of divine right is pointedly uncompelling; after his daughter's defiant top G, the king reaches only an anticlimactic E-flat before the wrath of Heaven falls on him: "Un fulmine scoppia sul capo del Re. Nabucodonosor atterrito sente strapparsi la corona da una forza soprannaturale." (155; A thunderbolt strikes the head of the king. Nabucodonosor, terrified, feels his crown torn off by a supernatural force.) Entering a world of delirium, Nabucco embarks on a tortuous voyage of self-discovery. His fragmented and rhythmically unsettled vocal line builds *incalzando* to a terrified, syncopated collapse as his kingly façade disintegrates: "Chi mi toglie il regio scettro?.. Qual m'incalza orrendo spettro?.. Chi pel crine, ohimè, m'afferra?.. chi mi stringe?.. chi m'atterra, chi, chi m'atterra, chi, chi m'atterra?" (158; Who takes the royal scepter from me? What horrible specter pursues me? Oh, who seizes me by the hair? Who grips me? Who throws me down?)

But, even in his confusion, Nabucco soon senses a loss greater than that of his crown, a profound void that threatens the true essence of his being.[10] With the tempo shifting fluidly into a lamenting *adagio espressivo*, his broken phrases are underscored by mournful woodwinds as he sobs, "Oh!.. mia figlia!.. e tu e tu pur anco non... soccorri al debil.. fianco?" (159; Oh my daughter!.. will even you not aid me in my weakness?).

chi? Oh!...... mia fi - glia!..e tu e tu pur an - co non...... soc - cor - ri al de - bil.... fian - co?...

Fueled by this torment, Nabucco's original hallucinations intensify, and the heightened *tessitura* of the Verdi baritone is now transformed into an expression of almost unbearable anguish at the loss of his daughter. Again and again the vocal line explodes to top F, only to plunge into an inferno of grief and horror: "Ah fantasmi ho sol presenti" (159; Ah, I have only phantoms around me). But out of this nightmare comes an instinctive understanding as Nabucco returns to a *dolce adagio*: "perchè... perchè sul... ciglio una lagrima, una lagrima spuntò?" (160; Why did a tear well up in my eye?). His conscious mind may not yet know what brings on this uncontrollable emotion, but his heart does. Subconsciously, he echoes the melody of "Oh mia figlia," the vocal line swelling with a need that defies articulate expression as it *crescendos* to top F on "ciglio."[11]

Ah perchè, perchè sul ci - glio u - na la - grima.... spun - tò?

At last Nabucco can bear his suffering no longer and sinks into a faint, a symbolic death from which he will ultimately be resurrected with a new and deeper understanding of himself and of the values that give true meaning to his life.

The Nabucco of Act III is a pathetic shadow of the arrogant monarch who ordered the sacking of the temple of Solomon.[12] Disheveled and distracted, he wanders like a stranger through his own throne room, his feeble efforts to maintain some vestige of royal authority subverted by his tentative and unfocused recitative: "Vo' che mi creda sempre forte ciascun" (172; I want everyone to think me still strong).[13] In the great duet "Donna, chi sei?" (173; Woman, who are you?), Nabucco is easily outmaneuvered by Abigaille, browbeaten into signing a death warrant for the Hebrews by her transparent mockery of his earlier self-image of power: "Preso da vil sgomento, Nabucco non è più" (176; Seized with cowardly fear, Nabucco is no more). Even his final effort to force Abigaille into submission by revealing her base birth is crushed as she destroys the incriminating document before his eyes, overwhelming his vocal line with a savage onslaught of fiendish *coloratura*.

The last shreds of pretense now drop away, and Nabucco recognizes that he has been stripped of the kingly role by which he has defined himself. With this new self-awareness, however, also comes new freedom of expression, and there is an unexampled emotional weight and majestic dignity in the *andante* "Oh di qual'onta." Nabucco has never seemed more regal than at the moment he recognizes that he is a king no longer. The sweeping phrases of his lament carry the vocal line first to a sobbing series of D-flats on "Oh di qual'onta aggravasi questo mio crin... canuto" and then to a surging E-flat on "Invan la destra gelida... corre all'acciar temuto." (179-80; Oh, what disgrace overwhelms my white hair. In vain my cold right hand now reaches for my feared sword.) At last, as words fail him, his sense of loss climaxes with a four-fold repetition of "l'ombra tu sei... del re" (180-81; You are the shadow of the king). It is left to the melodic line to capture the cry of his heart through the haunting elegance of a pair of triplets, the *stringendo* top F, and the *diminuendo* as the denouement fades into oblivion, just as Nabucco's kingship itself has drifted away.

l'om - bra tu sei...............del re,............... l'om-bra tu se - i, l'om-bra tu

se - i,.........................l'om - bra, l'ombra tu sei del re.

Abigaille answers his grief only with scorn, declaring Nabucco her prisoner. Like Shakespeare's Lear, Nabucco now understands that love, not power, is of paramount value in his life; prison holds no terrors as long as his daughter is saved. Returning to the original key of "Oh di qual'onta," Nabucco balances the loss of a crown with the return of paternal love. There is a new urgency in his *affettuoso allegro moderato* as he begins, "Deh perdona" (185-86; Ah, forgive). Abbreviated phrases, heightened with anxious triplets, emphasize his emotional tension as Nabucco freely casts aside his crown to plead for his daughter: "Te regina, te signora chiami pur... la gente assira; questo veglio non implora che la vita del... suo cor" (186; Let the people of Assyria call you queen and lady; this old man begs only for the life of his heart). But faced with Abigaille's contemptuous rejection of his pleas, he can only repeat his text in the second verse. At last, Nabucco is reduced to joining Abigaille on her musical terms, adopting her melodic lead in his plea for mercy, resigning himself to a subordinate role as she ascends to a high A-flat at the end of the duet, while he remains on middle A-flat. Nabucco has achieved a personal anagnorisis, recognizing that worldly power is dross compared with the richness of the love he shares with Fenena.

In the final act of the opera, this personal focus is expanded to provide a classical affirmation of humanity's place within a cosmic order of existence. Act IV opens with Nabucco asleep in a chair, and Verdi's prelude suggests the king's subconscious understanding of his downfall: the initial motif associated with his terror at being struck down by the hand of God thus gives way to melodic echoes of the Hebrews' pleas for mercy and Nabucco's triumphant conquest. In denying his own humanity, in turning a deaf ear to the claims of compassion and mercy, in trying to subordinate Earth and Heaven to his will, Nabucco has brought on his own self-destruction.

Significantly, however, it is the strength of his paternal love that ultimately propels Nabucco to a full conscious understanding of his hubris. He first awakens in a further delirium, calling on his troops to the sack Jerusalem. But the sight of Fenena, chained and weeping as she is led by his window to her execution, suddenly brings Nabucco back to reality: "Ah, prigioniero io sono" (213; Ah, I am a prisoner). Acknowledging his own grievous fault, the king humbles himself to the will of God, imploring, "Dio degli Ebrei, perdono" (213-14; Forgive me, God of the Hebrews). This acceptance of his place in a greater universal order immediately brings forgiveness and rebirth. The tempo shifts to *andante* as calm is restored, the strings return to the serene piety of Zaccaria's earlier prayer, and a flute *cadenza* shimmers like a ray of light in the darkness of a clouded mind.

Falling to his knees in complete submission to the God he now accepts as his own Lord, Nabucco begins his prayer with hesitant, fragmented phrases as he moves uncertainly into a new realm of personal faith and redefined self-identity: "Dio di... Giuda!.. l'ara, il tempio a te... sacro, a te sacro, sorgeranno" (214; God of Judah, the altar, the temple sacred to Thee shall rise anew). Without grandiose declamation, without personal pretense or bombast, Nabucco turns his thoughts and his heart to Heaven, his simple melody giving glory only to God with a leaping triplet on "te" and a fervent extension of "sorgeranno."

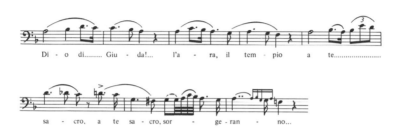

His vocal line weighted with pathos, Nabucco renounces his idolatrous past and pleads for release from his torment. His vocal line is doubled in the orchestra and rises to an *allargando* top E on "affanno," as Nabucco prays, "Mi togli a tanto affanno ei miei riti e miei riti struggerò" (214-15; Free me from such anguish, and my rites I will destroy). Yet, it is his new faith, not his past suffering, that dominates the prayer; the line returns to the leaping triplet figure of divine adoration, a sweeping ascent to a climactic top F on "riti," and a final surging series of dotted sixteenth notes that embody Nabucco's triumphant transcendence of the past.

Nabucco is now reborn, clarity and vigor flowing through his being like the stream of woodwinds that flows through the orchestration. Grief is transmuted into joy as he embraces the glory of God, true and omnipotent; the vocal line returns once more to the triplet motif, now elaborated with ever more fervent embellishments on a four-fold repetition of "adorarti ognor saprò" (215; I will worship Thee always).

When Nabucco approaches the door of his prison, it opens as if by divine intervention to reveal his loyal followers, who hail the return of their monarch and hand him his sword "Per acquistare il soglio" (217; to win the throne). But Nabucco is no longer concerned with power for its own sake: "Salvar Fenena io voglio" (217; I want to save Fenena).[14] With this affirmation of love, he achieves the strength and majesty that had before eluded him. Power and purpose now fuse, and his *cabaletta*, "O prodi miei, seguitemi," is a consummate statement of irresistible authority in its heightened *tessitura*, boldly self-assured repetition of top F's, and declamatory brass underscoring (218; Follow me, my gallant men).

The play of *Nabuchodonosor* ends with one final, gratuitous *coup de théâtre*: the king arrives too late to save Phénenna, only to see her raised from the dead by the power of God as Zacharie cries, "Où la puissance humaine s'arrête, la puissance divine commence... Toi, le plus grand roi de la terre, tu ne peux rien que pleurer ton enfant, regard ce que mon Dieu peut faire." (28; Where human power ends, divine power begins. You, the greatest king on earth, can do nothing but mourn your child, but look what my God can do.) The opera adopts a less bombastic, more psychologically insightful, conclusion that focuses not on the miraculous intervention of God but on the new life of a changed man.

Nabucco has saved his daughter and has seen the idol of Baal fall and shatter. His last moments in the opera are ones of beneficence and self-effacement; he frees the Hebrews and affirms that their God alone "è grande, è forte" (230; is great and powerful). Acknowledging that only through contrition comes peace, accepting that kings are still men who must embrace their mortal role in a larger order of existence, Nabucco touches on the tragic joy of the classical Greek drama. Out of suffering has come salvation, and as the ensemble gives voice to the hymn of praise "Immenso Jeovha" (231), Nabucco, with Fenena beside him, is content to become one of the crowd. He freely subordinates his own glory to that of Heaven and in doing so attains true majesty: "Servendo a Jeovha sarai de' regi il re" (240; Serving Jehovah, you will be the king of kings).[15]

Ernani

In many respects, Victor Hugo's *Hernani* seems particularly conducive to the kind of maudlin, romantic treatment stereotypically associated with operatic transformations. Despite its theatrical innovations, Hugo's drama is, above all, an emotionally expansive, lyrically poetic, vividly evocative celebration of the power of human love to transcend hatred and cruelty. Verdi's *Ernani* (1844), however, eschews many of the operatic clichés that might be expected in the adaptation of this play: the opera focuses not on Hugo's love story but on his exploration of the psychological development of Don Carlos, king of Spain.

Verdi's interest in *Hernani* was sparked by the play's action rather than its lyrical reflections, but in the opera, the composer goes beyond superficial theatricality to offer an incisive exploration of character.[1] Like much of early Verdi, *Ernani* has been criticized for its musical bombast and lack of sophistication; yet, while the opera is not without shortcomings, the musical characterization in *Ernani* is illuminating and dramatically insightful—shallow and bombastic as appropriate, but also subtle and delicate when needed for the character. Contemporary nineteenth-century reviewers noted the power of Verdi's portrayals: "Verdi has been unusually felicitous in his distribution of the vocal parts. The various characters are so musically individualised, and so peculiarly accompanied by the orchestra, that the voice of the singer becomes as easily recognisable by the *motivi*, as he does by his costume. To secure this is the highest achievement of the dramatic composer."[2]

If Verdi is to be criticized, it should perhaps be for his miscalculations in guiding his novice librettist, Francesco Maria Piave. Because of the selective compression of Hugo's play, the dramatic viability of Ernani, Elvira, and Silva is significantly undermined. Reduced to a pallid shadow of Hugo's exuberant protagonist, Ernani simply cannot rise above his image of weakness and melancholy to attain truly heroic stature. Although Elvira displays a dynamism more characteristic of early Verdian heroines than of the stereotypical operatic maiden, she is ultimately betrayed by the libretto's suppression of her *liebestod* at the end of the opera. And because of casting difficulties at the time of *Ernani's* composition, Hugo's central figure of Ruy Gomez is virtually eviscerated in the operatic adaptation, becoming the faintly sketched *comprimario*, Silva. As a result, it is Carlo who assumes dramatic preeminence in the opera, and it is Verdi's compelling use of the baritone voice to reveal the emotional nuances in Carlo's quest for self-identity that gives *Ernani* its most penetrating insights into the human condition.

The suppression of the original opening scene in Hugo's play is of particular importance to the operatic characterization of Carlo. Throughout the opening act of *Hernani*, Don Carlos maintains a certain sardonic distance from the romantic intrigues in which he is involved. Indeed, his initial response to Hernani's passionate exchange with Doña Sol is ironic and undercutting: "Quand aurez-vous fini de conter votre histoire?/ Croyez-vous donc qu'on soit à l'aise en cette armoire?" (When will you have done with recounting your story? Do you think it is comfortable in this armoire?)[3] His misadventures with Doña Sol's intractable duenna and his concealment in an absurdly small armoire at first place Don Carlos more in the tradition of comic libertine than enamored lover. The ludicrous nature of his antics, however, also clearly anticipates the more sinister degradations into which Don Carlos will be driven by his obsession with Doña Sol. And Don Carlos' behavior in this act further suggests that his later passion is a construct of his imagination, developing as much from the frustration of his royal will as from the sincerity of his emotions.

Verdi and Piave, in contrast, emphasize the real love that Carlo feels for Elvira, portraying him from the beginning as an ardent but spurned lover—tender, caressing, even imploring. In a letter to Piave, Verdi makes clear his intentions in Carlo's first scene: "Al momento in cui entra don Carlo io farei un duettino assai gentile e sviluppare un poco più l'amore di don

Carlo" (At the moment Don Carlo enters, I would make a tender little duet and develop his love a bit more).[4] Verdi anticipates this romantic portrayal in an introductory *adagio cantabile*
with *pianissimo* string underscoring and elegant ornamentation.
As Carlo declares, "Quel cor tentiamo... una sol volta ancora"
(Once more, let us try that heart),[5] there is more intensity of
feeling in his single arching phrase than is evident in Ernani's
entire opening aria.

Rebuffed by Elvira at every advance, Carlo evidences
flashes of a more violent potential. His hammering vocal line
jumps a fifth to a sustained F punctuated by *fortissimo* orchestration as he explodes, "E un masnadiero fai superbo del tuo cor"
(49-50; And you make a bandit arrogant in possessing your
heart). Yet, this brief outburst is quickly followed by a
renewed expression of tenderness and devotion in the expansive *andantino cantabile*, "Da quel dì" (50; From that day).
Drawing on both the dark color and the inherent strength of
the baritone's upper middle range, Verdi creates a richly
nuanced portrait of a dynamic lover, of a more vital lover, in
fact, than Ernani.

There is both elegance and ardor in Carlo's rising *legato*
phrases, building to an emotionally weighted sequence of
surging E-flats on "un primo amore" (51; a first love). The
emotional tension beneath his controlled exterior is evident,
however, in the unslurred, fragmented phrase "Cedi, Elvira"

(51; Yield, Elvira). Carlo quickly regains his composure, but his heightened feeling is suggested by the prominent use of moving sixteenth notes in the soothing line "puro amor da te desio" (51; I desire pure love from you).

Ce - di, El-vi - ra,   a' vo - ti   mie - - i;   pu -ro a - mor,   pu-ro amor da   te   de - - si - o;

Elvira vehemently rejects Carlo, obliterating the tender close of his declaration of love with a chilling series of explosive, plunging phrases: "Fiero sangue d'Aragona nelle vene a me trascorre... lo splendor... d'una corona leggi al cor, no,.. no, non puote imporre" (52; Proud blood of Aragon flows in my veins... the splendor of a crown cannot impose laws on my heart). Her melody dominates the beginning of the ensuing duet, overwhelming Carlo's futile protestations. His eventual adoption of her melodic line, however, goes beyond mere musical conventionality to suggest a subtle attempt to bridge the abyss between their two positions, to couch his appeal in terms Elvira will accept: "gioja e vita esser tu dêi" (53; You must be the joy and life). Yet, Carlo is not all conciliation, and his desire to reestablish control in the scene is evidenced by his return to a melodic echo of his earlier *andantino* (54).

In response to this new assertiveness, Elvira tempers her vehemence, picking up on Carlo's melody as the vocal lines intertwine, and this musical interplay suggests something more than unrelenting ferocity in Elvira. As in Hugo's original, it is love for Ernani rather than hatred of Carlo that motivates Elvira. Yet, despite this dynamic musical dialogue, the positions of Elvira and Carlo are ultimately irreconcilable, and the final *cadenza* of the duet emphasizes this divergence (56).

It is a telling indication of the fundamental shift away from romance in the focus of the opera that Ernani and Elvira are first brought together not for a love scene, as in Hugo's original, but for a moment of crisis and confrontation. His arrival to foil the kidnapping of his lover offers a striking opportunity for Ernani to establish himself as a more heroic and less meditative protagonist. Certainly Hugo's Hernani loses no time in taking control in both of his confrontations with Don Carlos; Ernani, in contrast, speaks only in concert with Elvira, their unison vocal lines subverting his domination of the situation (59).

The ensuing *allegro vivacissimo* trio, serving as the *cabaletta* for the duet between Elvira and Carlo, seems more reflective of her fiery personality than of Ernani's melancholy character. Ernani appears merely to join in her declaration of defiance, a subordination that is further emphasized when he is reduced to the harmonic line at critical moments in the trio (62). Carlo's response to this onslaught is initially disjointed, but it gains steadily in both force and confidence.

The finale of the first act is of note primarily for anticipating the values of mercy and virtue that will ultimately transfigure Carlo. In an extended discussion with Ruy Gomez of the impending election for the throne of the Holy Roman Empire, Hugo's Don Carlos emphasizes the *realpolitik* that guides his life. By contrast, Verdi's Carlo dispenses with political concerns in two brief lines to Silva: "Morte colse l'avo augusto, or si pensa al successore... La tua fè conosco e il core... vo'i consigli d'un fedel." (101-102; Death took my august ancestor, and now they are thinking of a successor. I know your heart and faith, and I want the counsel of a loyal man.) In an incisive moment of self-knowledge which is unfortunately obscured in the trivial bustle of the ensemble, Carlo's thoughts instead foreshadow his later metamorphosis: "La clemente giustizia e il valore meco ascendere in trono farò" (108-10; I will make merciful justice and valor ascend the throne with me).[6] In this context, Carlo's saving of Ernani also takes on more explicit significance than in Hugo's play; it becomes an indication of his capacity for imperial clemency.

This clemency is balanced in the second act, however, by Carlo's promise of apocalyptic retribution for Silva's betrayal. Piave's text for "Lo vedremo" is suitably brash, but Verdi's music provides a more subtly nuanced characterization. The menace in Carlo's *declamato* vocal line, underscored by ominously muted strings, is far more compelling than any verbal tirade, and the extended C-sharp on "vedremo" slows the musical momentum to create a sense of perilously suspended fury (175; We will see, audacious old man). Indeed, Carlo's violent potential is not fully exposed until the barking, accented sixteenth notes of "se resistermi potrai" (176; if you are able to resist me).

Another juxtaposition of restraint and explosion colors his next phrase, though Carlo evidences increasing difficulty in containing his anger. The vocal line mounts to a *con forza*, accented E underscored by *fortissimo* doubling orchestration as he obsessively repeats, "la vendetta, la vendetta del tuo re" (176; the vengeance, the vengeance of your king). He taunts Silva, "Essa rugge sul tuo capo," and the vocal line soon erupts in a chilling embodiment of implacable destruction, leaping a fifth to an accented, *con forza* F-sharp strengthened by heavy orchestral doubling: "pensa pria,.. pensa pria che tutta scenda" (176-77; It roars over your head; think before all falls upon you). The rising impetus within each pair of sixteenth notes in the final plunging phrase powerfully underscores Carlo's seething intensity.

pen-sa pri - - a, ... pensa pria che tutta scen - - da

The frustration Carlo feels at the defiance of his authority is only aggravated by Silva's dignified "No, de' Silva il disonore non vorrà d'Iberia un re" (177-78; No, a king of Spain will not want the dishonor of the Silvas). He simply cuts Silva off with the ultimatum, "Il tuo capo, o traditore... no, altro scampo no, non v'è, no, no, non v'è, no, no, non v'è" (178-79; Your head, o traitor... there is no other escape for you). The restrained menace of Carlo's earlier lines begins to collapse at this point, giving way to a *crescendo* of pounding C-sharps and climaxing with an accented E before a leaping, declamatory descent. When Silva repeats his protestations, Carlo's vocal line departs from the established melodic pattern to dominate the exchange with a sustained F-sharp on "traditore" (179). There is no further movement in his position, no attempt at manipulation. Rather, Carlo relentlessly asserts his personal power, culminat-

ing in the imperious ascent of his final *cadenza* and the intransi-
gent repetition of "no, no, no, no, non v'è" (180).

In the context of Hugo's play, Don Carlos' ruthless confrontation with Ruy Gomez, his hounding of Hernani, and his
abduction of Doña Sol are manifestations of his degradation,
the result of his obsessive passion: "C'est vous qui m'avez mis
au coeur cette colère./ Un homme devient ange ou monstre en
vous touchant." (1243; It is you who have put this anger in my
heart. A man becomes an angel or a monster in touching you.)
Gone is the sardonic distance with which Don Carlos could
view events in the opening scenes of the play, for the frustration of his will drives him to self-assertion by even the most
reprehensible means. The potential for good that love might
have nurtured in him is transformed into hatred and revenge.

Piave does not emphasize such degradation in his portrayal of Carlo, turning even the abduction of Elvira into a
tender act of devotion: "Vieni meco, sol di rose intrecciar ti vo'
la vita" (187; Come with me, I want to entwine your life only
with roses). Even given the public context of "Vieni meco,"
Carlo's delicate musical expression seems understated in comparison with the amorous intensity of "Da quel dì." There is a
feeling of soothing placation in the regularity of his four-mea-
sure phrases, static repetition of D, and elegant triplets.

Carlo is a man seeking a path through the confusion of his
passions and desires toward a greater sense of self-definition,

and his quest will ultimately culminate in the ascendence of the virtues of mercy and forgiveness that will bring him glory as Holy Roman Emperor. In the process, however, Carlo must not only overcome the temptation to use his power for domination and revenge but also sacrifice his hopes of love. Verdi's musical characterization in "Vieni meco" provides a subtle and touching insight into this transformation. Although there is a hint of Carlo's underlying romantic yearning in the building musical phrases of "Tergi il pianto, o giovinetta, dalla guancia scolorita," a feeling of distance from Elvira, and even resignation to her loss, dominates (187; Wipe the tears, o maiden, from your pale cheek). Carlo may still hope to win her, but he also seems to sense that his dream is slipping away. His awareness that taking Elvira with him through coercion will not achieve the love he seeks is suggested by the almost plaintive futility in his reprise of "Vieni meco." Carlo is unable to infuse his words with any new resonance that might gain her affection.

In both the play and the opera, Carlo finally achieves a true sense of self in his great scene at Charlemagne's tomb.[7] As he awaits the election for the crown of the Holy Roman Empire, Hugo's Don Carlos is forced to confront his own ambition, forced to recognize that power for its own sake is meaningless. With supreme secular power almost in his grasp, Don Carlos acknowledges, for the first time, the responsibilities of such power and evaluates his own fitness to wield it. As he assesses his values and aspirations, Don Carlos looks deep into his own soul, and the sight is humbling:

> —Puis, quand j'aurai ce globe entre mes mains,
>   qu'en faire?
> Le pourrai-je porter seulement? Qu'ai-je en moi?
> Être empereur, mon Dieu! j'avais trop d'être roi!

Certe, il n'est qu'un mortel de race peu commune
Dont puisse s'élargir l'âme avec la fortune.
Mais, moi! qui me fera grand? qui sera ma loi?
Qui me conseillera? Charlemagne! c'est toi!
   [1265]

Then, when I have the globe in my hands, what
to do with it? Will I be able to carry it alone? Do
I have it in me? To be emperor, my God! I have
had too much being king! Indeed, it is only an
uncommon mortal who is able to enlarge his
spirit along with his fortunes. But I, who will
make me great? who will be my law? who will
counsel me? Charlemagne! It is you!

Significantly, however, Don Carlos enters Charlemagne's
tomb still searching for answers, still unclear about the path
that will lead him to true glory.

Piave's Carlo, in contrast, evidences a much greater degree
of self-knowledge. There is no sense in him of petty obsession
with the politics of empire and, indeed, no sudden moment of
discovery. Piave portrays a monarch who has already sur-
mounted temptation and set his course toward transcendence.
Long before he arrives at Charlemagne's tomb, Carlo has
begun to sense the inadequacy of the values that have guided
his life, and this sense finds full expression in Verdi's mournful
prelude to Act IV. Carlo shows little interest in the upcoming
election, dismissing Riccardo with a brusk, "Lo so... mi lascia"
(222-23; I know... leave me). His thoughts are already else-
where.

Carlo recognizes his desire for immortality. Through the
legend of his name, he can transcend death itself, and it is
with this understanding that he discards the more transitory
lures of existence. The emotional strain in rejecting his youth-

ful vision of life is clear in the lunging phrases, accelerating pace, and rising pitch of the vocal line as he questions, "Scettri!.. dovizie!.. onori!.. bellezze!.. gioventù!.. che siete voi?" (224; Scepters! wealth! honors! beauty! youth! what are you?). But with this catharsis, a new serenity and noble calm descend. There is a somber eloquence in the phrases of his *andante con moto*, underscored by a chamber music accompaniment of cellos and double bass. Fluid ornamentation and a narrow vocal range negate Carlo's early feeling of torment and highlight his new understanding, "Oh de' verd'anni miei sogni e bugiarde larve, se troppo vi credei, l'incanto, l'incanto ora disparve" (225; Oh dreams and false phantoms of my youthful years, if I believed in you too much the spell has now disappeared).

Yet, Carlo's triumph lies in his ability to go beyond an understanding of the past to embrace a vital new image of the future. As he envisions his transfiguration as emperor, his vocal line takes on a swelling intensity, straining, like Carlo himself, to break free of temporal constraints: "S'ora chiamato sono al più sublime trono" (225-26; If now I am called to the most sublime throne). Although he emphasizes "della virtù com'aquila sui vanni, sui vanni m'alzerò" (226; on the wings of virtue, like an eagle I will rise), it is the immortality that such virtue will bring that provides the emotional climax to Carlo's thoughts. Accelerating *con un poco più di moto* and doubled for the first time by the orchestra, his vocal line *crescendos* through an extended C to erupt into the sweeping, *con forza* phrases of "e vincitor de' secoli il nome... il nome mio farò" (226; and will make my name conqueror of the centuries). An accented F emphasizes the key phrase "il nome," which is repeated on an urgent series of propulsive sixteenth notes, doubled by the orchestra. As Carlo repeats this vision of triumph, his vocal line culminates in a majestic rise to a sustained E-flat that bursts, with a final surge of passionate energy, to G-flat before a deliberate descent (227). Carlo's unrequited love for Elvira cannot offer such transfiguration, and the contrast in musical vitality between "Vieni meco" and "Oh de' verd'anni miei" vividly reveals the ascendence of a dominant new life force.[8]

e vin - ci - tor de'   se - - co- li il nome mio fa - rò.........il nome mi - - - - o   fa - rò.

Although Carlo at first reacts with his ingrained desire for revenge at the unmasking of the conspirators, he soon reconciles his conduct with his new ideals. In Hugo's original, Don Carlos' clemency is a *coup de théâtre*, the inspiration of Charlemagne divulged only at the end of the act: "Je t'ai crié:—Par où faut-il que je commence?/ Et tu m'as répondu:—Mon fils, par la clémence." (1286; I cried to you:—Where should I begin? And you responded:—My son, with clemency.) In Piave's adaptation, self-knowledge takes precedence over dramatic suspense, and Carlo reveals his thoughts even as he makes his decision: "Oh sommo Carlo, più del tuo nome le tue virtudi... aver vogl'io" (253; O supreme Carlo, more than your name, I wish to have your virtues). Underscored by shimmering harp arpeggios, Carlo's noble *adagio* is enhanced by the darker colors of the baritone's middle and lower registers. In his majestically weighted, arching phrases, Carlo seems reborn, able to rise above the turbulence and trials of his past life and the temptation of his own darker nature. There is no sense here, or in the ensuing ensemble, of any personal loss that Carlo must endure in his pursuit of majesty. The sacrifice of Hugo's Don Carlos in renouncing his claim to love is glossed over in Piave's text, and Carlo ascends in untroubled apotheosis.[9]

Ernani ultimately reveals not the power of love but the dynamics of kingship and the quest for self-identity embodied in Carlo. His absence from the final act, therefore, is dramatically anticlimactic. Neither Ernani nor Elvira has been portrayed with the subtlety and insight of Carlo's characterization, and even their love has been little more than an abstract ideal without sustained dramatic development. The powerful scenes that bring the relationship of Hugo's Hernani and Doña Sol to life are suppressed in the opera, and it is hardly surprising, therefore, that the emotional climax of that relationship lacks real resonance.

The love of Ernani and Elvira simply does not have the all-consuming, transcendent power that possesses Doña Sol and Hernani. In the face of hatred and malevolence, their love is too fragile to endure, much less triumph. What for Doña Sol and Hernani becomes a new beginning, a "nuit de noce" (1319; wedding night), marks the end for Verdi's lovers: "Per noi d'amore il talamo... di morte fu l'altar" (297; For us the nuptial bed of love was the altar of death). It is a chilling negation of Hugo's Romantic vision, culminating in Elvira's collapse over the body of her dead lover, while Silva, like an incarnation of all destructive human hatred, victoriously invokes his evil god: "Delle vendette il demone qui venga ad esultar" (297; Let the demon of vengeance come here to exult). At least one nineteenth-century staging of the opera, however, tried to counter the desolation of this haunting scene, bringing down the curtain on an image of hope rather than despair, as the triumphant new emperor and his retinue return to the stage for the final tableau: "À ce moment, entre Charles suivi des choeurs figuration" (At this moment Carlo enters, followed by a chorus of extras).[10]

Macbeth

Verdi's first Shakespearean opera, *Macbeth* (1865),[1] marks a new level of subtlety and sophistication in the composer's dramatic exploration of the human condition. For all its fantastical trappings—witches, apparitions, and mysterious prophecies—Shakespeare's *Macbeth* is a profoundly humanistic drama from which Verdi creates a stunning operatic exploration of the individual psyche, of the psychological ramifications of human action, and of the personal cost of hubris. Indeed, in the characterization of Macbeth, the opera offers a haunting indictment of what, later in the century, Nietzsche would celebrate as the Will to Power.

Critics have often reviled Verdi's *Macbeth* as a travesty of the Shakespeare play, the brunt of their opprobrium falling on the librettist, Piave.[2] But it was Verdi himself who conceived and executed the operatic adaptation of *Macbeth*, fusing words and music in the creation of a powerfully unified artistic vision: "Sono or dieci anni, mi venne in capo di fare il *Macbeth*: ne feci io stesso la selva; anzi più della selva, feci distesamente il dramma in prosa, colla distribuzione di atti, scene, pezzi ecc., ecc.; poi lo diedi a Piave da verseggiare." (Ten years ago now, it came into my head to do *Macbeth*: I did the scenario of it myself, and even more than the scenario I wrote the drama in detail in prose, with the arrangement of acts, scenes, numbers etc., etc.; then I gave it to Piave to versify.)[3]

Macbeth was envisioned as a unified music-drama in which the dominance of traditional *bel canto* composition and vocal performance yielded to the supremacy of words and dramatic truth. Even in casting, dramatic values were primary for Verdi, who insisted on having Felice Varesi in the title role: "Nessun attore, al presente, in Italia può fare più bene il *Macbeth* di Varesi, e per il suo modo di canto, e per la sua intelligenza, e per la sua stessa piccola e brutta figura. Forse egli dirà che stuona, questo non fa niente perchè la parte sarebbe quasi tutta declamata, ed in questo vale molto." (No actor at present in Italy can do *Macbeth* better than Varesi, on account of his way of singing, his intelligence, and even his small and ugly figure. Perhaps one will say that he sings out of tune, but that means nothing because the role would be almost entirely declaimed, and he is good at that.)[4] And Verdi himself wrote to Varesi, "Io non cesserò mai di raccomandarti di studiare bene la posizione, e le parole; la musica viene da se. Insomma ho più piacere che servi meglio il poeta del maestro." (I will never cease to implore you to study well the dramatic context and words; the music comes by itself. In short, it pleases me more for you to serve the poet than the composer.)[5]

Verdi's *Macbeth* is far from a slavish musical setting of Shakespeare's play. Following the dictum "POCHE PAROLE" (few words),[6] Verdi further accelerates Shakespeare's headlong drama, jettisoning some of the richness and nuance of the play, distilling from Shakespeare an essentially classical tragedy of human hubris. The composer's outrage at one French review of the opera testifies to Verdi's own sense of dramatic fidelity: "Chi trova che io non conosco Shacpeare [*sic*] quando scrissi il *Macbeth*. Oh, in questo hanno un gran torto. Può darsi che non abbia reso bene il *Macbeth*, ma che io non conosco, che non capisco e non sento Shaspeare [*sic*] no, per Dio, no. È un poeta di mia predilezione, che ho avuto fra le mani dalla mia prima gioventù, e che leggo e rileggo continuamente." (One finds that I did not know my Shakespeare when I wrote *Macbeth*. Oh, in this they are very wrong. It may be said that I have not rendered *Macbeth* well, but that I do not know, understand, and feel Shakespeare, no, by God, no! He is one of my favorite poets, whom I have had in my hands since my earliest youth, and whom I read and reread continually.)[7]

Like *Nabucco*, *Macbeth* is an exploration of the fatal arrogance that leads a man to anoint himself master of a cosmic order beyond his control. Macbeth's hubris transcends the easy cliché of ambition: his downfall results not from his desire for a crown but from his desire to take control of his own destiny, to achieve a power beyond mortal grasp. The dramatic focus of the opera is internal and psychological— exploring the mind of one individual, tracing his decisions and the repercussions of those decisions, not in society at large but within his own psyche. The world of the opera is proto-expressionistic, the fantastical becoming an embodiment of the dark recesses of his mind as Macbeth enters a nightmare of his own making.

In contrast to *Nabucco*, the ideals of religious faith are absent from this opera; there is no possibility of repentance and forgiveness for Macbeth. Instead, the opera traces a path of irreversible self-destruction, powerfully transplanting the inexorability of Greek tragedy into the Romantic realm of the individual's inner self. Macbeth believes "he can turn the wheel on which he turns."[8] He proclaims individual Will as his ultimate power and the only guide to his conduct; but his extravagant self-affirmation leads only to torment, loss, and meaninglessness. In *Macbeth* there are no last-minute reprieves. The consequences of actions take their relentless human toll. Yet, out of the very desolation of Macbeth's life comes a greater understanding of mortal limitations and the sources of meaning in human existence.

From the opening of the opera, Macbeth is unmoored from the socio-historical context that anchors him in the first scenes of Shakespeare's play. By stripping away his exploits in battle, the accolades of his king, the respect of his comrades at arms, Verdi imbues Macbeth with a new symbolic resonance as an embodiment of humanity at large; he insists that the primary focus of the opera will be the inner world of the individual rather than the social world in which he lives. Macbeth is conceived as a type of Everyman, faced with a fateful decision that will shape the rest of his life: whether, like Banco, to accept the course of destiny, or to take an active role in effecting that destiny.

Verdi immediately brings the drama to bear on this central issue as the witches hail Macbeth Thane of Glamis, Thane of Cawdor, and King of Scotland. Despite such happy tidings, however, Macbeth feels neither joy nor elation; rather, the thought of murder flashes into his mind, and the stage directions indicate, "Macbeth trema" (Macbeth trembles).[9] With the arrival of messengers announcing, "Pro Macbetto, il tuo signore sir t'elesse di Caudore" (20; Brave Macbeth! Your sovereign has elevated you to Thane of Cawdor), Macbeth is poised at the edge of the abyss, the glitter of Scotland's crown before him.

As he murmurs *quasi con ispavento*, "Due vaticini compiuti or sono" (21; Two prophecies are now fulfilled), the fragmented vocal line with its unsettled dotted rhythms and restless string accompaniment captures Macbeth's breathless anxiety. Passing quickly over the prophecies already fulfilled, Macbeth focuses on the horror of his own potential for evil, on the unspoken crime of murder. At the violent outburst of "Ma perchè sento," the vocal line leaps a sixth to a heavily accented series of E-flats marked *con esclamazione* before the terrified *cupo* whisper of "rizzarsi il crine," with its recoiling vocal descent and nervous dotted-sixteenth-note figures (21; But why do I feel my hair stand on end?). Macbeth knows all too well why his very being is consumed with horror, and he cries, "Pensier di sangue, d'onde sei nato?" (21; Bloody thought, from whence are you born?). The connection between "Ma perchè sento" and "Pensier di sangue" is accentuated by a repetition of the melodic pattern in the vocal line, now pitched down a tone as an indication of Macbeth's further retreat into the recesses of his own consciousness.

The vocal line takes on a new melodic expansiveness, and a *voce aperta* marking suggests Macbeth's return to clear conscience with the resolution "Alla corona che m'offre il fato la man rapace non alzerò" (21-22; I will not raise a grasping hand toward the crown that Fate offers me). The more *legato*

phrases, rising evenly to a top F, become a musical embodiment of his noble potential, a glimpse of the man Macbeth might have been. For a moment, he renounces the desire to control his own destiny; the intertwining of the individual lines in his ensuing duet with Banco thus takes on added significance, underscoring the bond that Macbeth is maintaining with the rest of humanity. Yet, there is also an undercurrent of continuing inner struggle in Macbeth's line, a hint of emotional upheaval as his voice rises *con slancio* to a top F on the repetition of "d'onde sei nato" (24), a hint of desperation in the seven-fold variation on "la man rapace non alzerò," which concludes on a *fortissimo* sustained F. The innate Will to Power is not easily denied.

Shakespeare provides an external motivation for Macbeth's decision to act: in Duncan's elevation of Malcolm to Prince of Cumberland, Macbeth recognizes "a step/ On which I must fall down, or else o'er-leap,/ For in my way it lies" (I.iv.48-50).[10] For Verdi's Macbeth, there is no external imperative, no second thought, and no coercion by Lady Macbeth. With the elimination of the tortured soliloquy "If it were done, when 'tis done, then 'twere well/ It were done quickly" (I.vii.1-2) and Macbeth's determined "We will proceed no further in this business" (I.vii.31), there is no need for Lady Macbeth to goad a reluctant husband to murder. His motivation comes entirely from within himself, and it cannot be ascribed simply to a lust for the throne, since no action by Duncano impedes the fulfillment of the witches' prophecy. Macbeth has no reason to doubt that chance will crown him without his stir, yet he will not wait. He greets his wife with murder already in his mind and raises only the most perfunctory concern of practical failure: "E se fallisse il colpo?" (49; And if the blow should fail?). There is no cause for Lady Macbeth's doubts, "alla grandezza aneli... ma sarai tu malvagio?" (36; You desire greatness, but will you be wicked?). Theirs is a meeting of the minds, and the decision to assassinate Duncano is reached in a scene lasting just over a minute in performance.

Although Macbeth embraces murder, he is still a man capable of horror at his own planned atrocities; his Will to Power may guide his acts, but it has not destroyed his moral conscience. Verdi's dramatic compression at this moment highlights the psychological effect of Macbeth's decision, for only the pantomimed arrival of Duncano separates Macbeth's bloody thoughts from the terrifying chimera of the Dagger Scene. In a breathless *sotto voce e cupa* recitative, punctuated by orchestration embodying the hallucinatory movements of the dagger, Verdi provides a powerful image of a man driven back onto the shoals of his own mind: "Mi si affaccia un pugnal?" (54-55; Is this a dagger that appears before me?). Underscored with shifting textures of strings, woodwinds, timpani, and brass, the vision of the dagger casts a hypnotic spell, ensnaring Macbeth with the insidious power of his own darkest impulses: "A me precorri sul confuso cammin che nella mente di seguir disegnava" (55-56; You lead me down the twisted path that, in my mind, I had resolved to follow). In a sudden flash of terror, Macbeth struggles to escape his stupor, bursting into a violent, *fortissimo allegro* cry, "Orrenda immago" (56; Horrible image). He is again transfixed, however, his *adagio* vocal line mounting slowly to a *fil di voce* C-sharp as he envisions Duncano's blood—the blood of his friend, his king, his guest—flowing from the assassin's blade: "Solco sanguigno la tua lama irriga" (56; A bloody furrow waters your blade).

Macbeth recognizes the dagger as a projection of his own bloody thoughts, but he cannot free himself. His *misterioso* vocal line flattens into an eerie monotone, underscored by increasingly otherworldly woodwind orchestration, as he whispers, "Sulla metà del mondo or morta è la natura: or l'assassino come fantasma per l'ombre si striscia" (57; Over half the world, nature is now dead: now the assassin creeps like a specter through the shadows). Here is a ghastly world of inhumanity, betrayal, and murder; a world of unspeakable atrocities, a world of darkness and alienation, a world in which the assassin is king. But despite the horror of this vision, Macbeth does not fully understand the implications of his hallucination. He refuses to recognize that through murder he will gain control only of an existence as desolate and meaningless as his imagined realm. Macbeth chooses this nightmare, assuming the identity of the faceless murderer as he prays, "a' passi miei sta muta" (57; May my steps be silent).

With the sound of the signal bell, Macbeth blindly rushes to his destruction in an act of tragic hubris. Underscored with orchestration weighted by full brass and timpani, the vocal line rises *a voce spiegato* to a top F in a proclamation of irre-

sistible power: "È squillo eterno che nel cielo ti chiama o nel-
l'inferno" (58; It is the final knell that summons you to Heaven
or to Hell). Macbeth virtually shouts down his own humanity,
but he remains a man fundamentally divided against himself. It
is thus fitting that the violent phrase on "inferno," leaping a
sixth to a D-flat extended by a fermata, not only gives a particular weight to the call of Hell, but also suggests the effort
by which Macbeth asserts the demonic sway of his own Will
to Power.

When Macbeth emerges from Duncano's chamber
moments later, he is on the verge of emotional collapse. His
headlong stichomythic duet with Lady Macbeth, "Fatal mia
donna" (59; My fateful wife), is a disjointed, *sotto voce* expression of panic, the voices swept along by the churning current
of the *allegro* orchestration just as Macbeth himself is propelled
by the maelstrom of events he has precipitated.[11] The
Nietzschean Superman who defiantly embraced murder is
now almost speechless with terror, repeating "Oh vista orri-
bile" (60; Oh horrible sight) three times to the same melodic
pattern, unable to tear his eyes away from his bloody hands.

He is damned by his own actions, and, as Macbeth
recounts how he was unable to say "Amen" to the courtiers'
prayers, he becomes fully aware of his irredeemable self-cor-
ruption. The nightmare is more terrifying than anything
Macbeth conceived, and it is centered not in a nameless world

of desolation, but within himself. Surging emotionality heightens the original melodic statement of the vocal line, as Macbeth cries out in anguish, "Perchè, perchè ripetere quell'*Amen* non potei?" (61-62; Why, why could I not repeat that 'Amen'?). Finally, with a *crescendo* underscored by ominous brass and woodwinds and building to a crushing series of accented F's, Macbeth recognizes his own irretrievable loss: "Il sonno per sempre, Glamis uccidesti! Non v'è che vigilia Caudore, per te" (63; Glamis has murdered sleep forever! There is nothing but waking for you, Cawdor).

Macbeth has seized the throne destiny offered, but his victory has a hollow ring. The murder of Duncano only forces Macbeth to recognize the unbridgeable chasm that separates his own baseness from the nobility of the slain king. It is thus fitting that Macbeth's moment of greatest melodic expansiveness in the scene comes in tribute to Duncano: "Com'angeli d'ira, vendetta tuonarmi udrò di Duncano le sante virtù" (64-65; I will hear Duncan's holy virtues thunder for vengeance like angels of wrath). His soaring phrases become a pathetic expression of the nobility that Macbeth himself has forfeited forever, an inescapable understanding of loss that reverberates relentlessly in his mind as he repeats broken, *sotto voce* fragments of melody before sinking into enervated paralysis.

com' an - ge - li d'i - ra,   u - drò di Dun-ca - no le san - te vir - tù...

Left alone on stage while Lady Macbeth returns with the incriminating dagger to besmear Duncano's guards with blood,

Macbeth makes his despairing recognition, "Oh questa mano!
non potrebbe l'Oceano queste mani a me lavar" (68-69; Oh this
hand! The ocean could not wash these hands clean). With
pointed irony, the vocal line echoes that of "È squillo eterno,"
but the melodic contours are now flattened and stripped of
orchestral support; the torment of indelible corruption is all
that Macbeth has gained from his Will to Power. Adrift in a
void of alienation and despair, tortured by a defilement that can
never be cleansed, Macbeth finds that victory has turned to ash.

Upon her return, Lady Macbeth assumes the dominant
role both dramatically and musically in the conclusion of the
scene. Macbeth, in a state of emotional paralysis, can only
reiterate his wife's melodic line, transforming her descending
eighth-note patterns into surging, ascending figures of helpless remorse that culminate in the crushing collapse of a sev-
enth: "Oh potessi il mio delitto dalla mente cancellar" (70;
Would that I could erase my crime from my mind). At last,
Macbeth's line breaks down completely into sobbing fragmentation, and Verdi notes, "sul finire dovrà appena appena sen-
tirsi la parola mentre Macbet (quasi fuori di se) è trascinato da
Lady" (At the end one should scarcely hear the words while
Macbeth [almost beside himself] is dragged away by Lady
Macbeth).[12]

The ability of Shakespeare's Macbeth to maintain the initiative to action after Duncan's murder, killing the grooms and

declaring with righteous fury, "Who could refrain,/ That had a heart to love, and in that heart/ Courage to make 's love known" (II.iii.116-18), is unthinkable in the opera. Macbeth is incapable of independent action. Instead, Lady Macbeth guides him like a sleepwalker through a ritual expression of horror and shock. He speaks only in unison with her or in conjunction with some other member of the ensemble at the close of the act. His bloody self-affirmation has led, ironically, only to self-negation.

Strains of the "Fatal mia donna" melody in the orchestral introduction to the second act recall not only the assassination itself but also the psychological torment that Macbeth, with the passage of time, is determined to suppress. Paralleling his first encounter with his wife, Macbeth enters already determined to pursue the murder of Banco and his son. He has fulfilled the witches' prophecy of kingship, but this victory is not enough. He cannot rest until the entire course of his destiny is subordinated to his Will. The witches' prophecy that Banco will be father to a line of kings mocks Macbeth, insisting on a fate beyond his ability to control. With volcanic, surging phrases of almost uncontrollable frustration set against a thickening orchestration, Macbeth cries, "Dunque i suoi figli regneran? Duncano per costor sarà spento?" (109; Then shall his sons reign? Shall Duncan have been killed for them?) He determines to change fate, and his recourse once more is murder; the melody of "È squillo eterno" echoes again in subconscious recognition of this second act of hubris, as Macbeth triumphantly cries, "Banco, l'eternità... t'apre il suo regno" (110; Banco, eternity opens its kingdom for you).

Yet, paradoxically, the more Macbeth struggles to grasp control over destiny, the more diminished in stature he

becomes. Shakespeare's Macbeth alone dominates the planned
assassination of Banquo, probing his friend's pliability, weigh-
ing the implications of the witches' prophecy, skillfully manip-
ulating the murderers, and pointedly excluding Lady Macbeth
from involvement in his plot: "Be innocent of the knowledge,
dearest chuck,/ Till thou applaud the deed" (III.ii.45-46).
Verdi's compression of these scenes into a single brief recitative elevates Lady Macbeth to the status of a full partner in the
crime. It is she who dominates the scene through her great
aria, "La luce langue," the text of which is ironically drawn
from lines spoken by Shakespeare's Macbeth (111; The light
wanes). She seems to drain away Macbeth's very essence, leaving her husband a hollow shell, reducing him to a supporting
player in his latest moment of self-affirmation.

By the banquet scene, it is clear that Macbeth's Will has
become stronger, but so too has the tortured response of his
conscience, his heart, his humanity. Macbeth confidently
takes the initiative in his public performance, greeting his
guests with a jovial *allegro brillante* that reveals no inner turmoil
over the murder he has ordered, and responding with
detached impassivity to the news of Banco's death. Yet, this
measured self-control cannot banish his hallucinations as
Banco's bloody ghost appears at the banquet table.[13] Macbeth's
initial response is a nearly schizophrenic combination of defiance and guilty evasion. The *fortissimo* outburst as Macbeth
demands of his guests, "di voi chi ciò fece," on a declamatory
series of F's is thus stripped of orchestral weight and reduced
to an anticlimactic repetition of A-flats, as he cries to Banco's
ghost, "Non dirmi ch'io fossi" (140-41; Which of you did this?
[to the ghost] Do not say I did it). This retreat continues in
the cringing chromaticism of "le ciocche cruento non

scuotermi incontro," though there is still a flash of defiance in
the octave leap to a top F on "incontro" (141-42; Do not shake
your bloody locks at me).

Macbeth makes a supreme effort to regain his self-control
as Lady Macbeth hisses, "E un uomo voi siete?" (Are you a
man?). His vocal line takes on new force and melodic definition, ascending to an F-flat underscored by strings and brass,
as he declares, "Lo sono ed audace s'io guardo tal cosa che al
demone stesso farebbe spavento" (142-43; I am, and a bold
one if I look upon a thing that would make the devil himself
afraid). It is an effort that leaves him at the edge of consciousness, his frantic repetitions ending in a fainting *diminuendo* on
"là... là" (143; there... there). But defiance reasserts itself as
Macbeth confronts the ghost, his hammering line making a
crescendo to a *fortissimo* high G-flat underscored by brass and
concluding *risoluto un poco accelerando*: "il sepolcro può render gli
uccisi? può render, può render gli uccisi?" (144; Can the grave
yield up its dead?).

As the ghost disappears, Macbeth tries to recapture the
jovial spirit of the banquet, but a lack of vitality is discernable
in his vocal line. Nonetheless, he now challenges both the
ghost and, implicitly, his own conscience, as he offers the
salutation "nè Banco obbliate, che lungi è... tuttor" (145; And
do not forget Banco, who is still far away). His defiance brings
only renewed torment, however, for the ghost reappears.
Interrupting the chorus' verse of the *brindisi*, Macbeth's frenzied
shouts, broken with panic, rise over *fortissimo allegro agitato*
orchestration to a *tutta forza* top E: "Va! Spirto d'abisso!..
Spalanca una fossa, o terra, l'ingoia... Fiammeggian quell'ossa."
(149-50; Go! Spirit of the abyss! Open a grave, o earth, and
swallow him. Engulf those bones in flames.) Just as after the

murder of Duncan, Macbeth is transfixed by the unspeakable terror of his vision. Hypothetical defiance becomes no more than an acknowledgment of present helplessness as he cries, "diventa pur tigre, leon minaccioso... m'abbranca... Macbetto tremar non vedrai" (151-52; Become a tiger, menacing lion... grasp me... you will not see Macbeth tremble). Finally, all resistance collapses with a reeling repetition of "fuggi!" on a series of monotone D's (152; Begone!).

Shakespeare's Macbeth fully understands that his hallucinations are the product of a soul not yet inured to the horrors of his deeds, and he determines to fare forward because no other course is open to him: "I am in blood/ Stepped in so far that, should I wade no more,/ Returning were as tedious as go o'er" (III.iv.168-70). In contrast, Verdi's Macbeth shows no such understanding. He willfully misconstrues the concept of "blood will have blood" (III.iv.153), implicitly offering the ghost the blood of another victim and determining once again to bend destiny to his Will: "Sangue a me... quell'ombra chiede, e l'avrà, l'avrà, lo giuro! il velame del futuro alle streghe, alle streghe squarcierò" (154-55; That ghost demands blood of me and shall have it, I swear. Through the witches I will tear off the veil of the future).

After the trauma Macbeth has endured, this reassertion of control demands a supreme effort, and as he begins "Sangue a me," his fragmented, tortured vocal line is marked *cupo* and *sotto voce*. But the line soon takes on new energy through the introduction of propulsive triplet figures that carry Macbeth to a *con forza* top F-sharp on "streghe squarcierò" (155-56). It is a compelling psychological statement, but one unfortunately overshadowed by the dramatic anomaly of a conventionally static finale: Macbeth and his wife incongruously reveal their

thoughts before the assembled chorus, which expresses at
length its fears at the sinister implications of the scene.

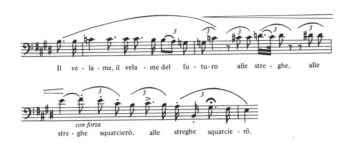

Il ve - la - me, il vela - me del fu - tu-ro   alle stre - ghe,   alle
stre - ghe squarcierò. alle streghe squarcie - rò.

con forza

When Macbeth arrives at the witches' cave in the third
act, he is resolved to impose his Will regardless of cost. His
pounding vocal line rises relentlessly to an extended E-flat as
Macbeth cries with anarchistic egocentrism, "io vi scongiuro!
ch'io sappia il mio destin, se cielo e terra dovessero innovar
l'antica guerra" (210; I conjure you to know my destiny,
though Heaven and Earth resume their ancient battle). The
witches oblige, but while Macbeth arrogantly undertakes to
command the spirits that rise up before him, they, like destiny
itself, are ultimately beyond his control.

The apparitions' warning to beware of Macduff, coupled
with the ensuing assurance "nessun nato di donna ti nuoce"
(213; None born of woman shall harm you), elicits a quicksil-
ver response from Macbeth that echoes Shakespeare's play.
Initial relief and willingness to spare Macduff's life are
instantly submerged, for Macbeth will not wait for destiny to
assure his safety: "No! no! no! no!.. morrai! Sul regale mio
petto doppio usbergo sarà." (214; No, you will die. It will be
double armor on my royal breast.) The chromatic ascent of his

repeated "no" culminates in an extended C-sharp, which is
repeated after a violent leap of an octave. But this dynamic
evocation of raw strength is followed by a shift away from
sweeping phrases and toward a hammering series of *staccato*
eighths and accented quarter notes that introduces a forced
tone of calculated fury. It is not real fear that leads Macbeth to
bloody thoughts but the imperative of his own Will to Power.

The zenith of Macbeth's quest for power comes with the
prophecy "glorïoso, invincibil sarai fin che il bosco di Birna
vedrai ravvïarsi e venir contro te" (215; You shall be glorious
and invincible until you see Birnam Wood come against you).
His desire to control destiny as an ultimate expression of his
personal supremacy is an end in itself, however, and with
invincibility assured Macbeth seems strangely adrift. His joy is
clear in the *allegro* exhilaration of "Oh! lieto augurio" (215-16;
Oh, happy augury), but the ascent to true glory and majesty
that inspires the new emperor's "O sommo Carlo" in *Ernani* is
not for Macbeth. Instead, there is only "vento e suono che
nulla dinota" (281; sound and fury signifying nothing).

At last Macbeth demands that the witches reveal the
future of Banco's progeny. As a procession of spectral kings
rises from the ground, Macbeth becomes virtually paralyzed

with disbelief. The first king is dismissed with a declamatory "Fuggi regal fantasima" (219-20; Fly, royal phantom), but the implacable procession drains Macbeth of his strength, relentlessly affirming the royal succession of Banco's heirs. His lines become increasingly fragmentary until Macbeth can only watch in silence as the last of the kings and Banco himself appear.[14] Seeing in Banco's mirror an endless line of kings, Macbeth erupts with helpless frustration, turning once more to the bloody deeds that have come to embody the strength of his own Will. Raising his sword against the apparitions, Macbeth cries, "Muori, fatal progenie" (224; Die, fateful progeny), his vocal line rising *con un grido* from three top F's to an accented G in a last desperate assertion of power. But unlike Duncano and Banco, the apparitions cannot be harmed.

Macbeth has made the negation of the witches' prophecy about Banco's royal heirs a test of his own ability to control destiny, and in a sudden moment of anagnorisis he is compelled to recognize his own human limitations. The mounting despair in a four-fold repetition of "che non hai tu vita" (224; But you have not life) thus culminates in an almost inarticulate "oh terror" (225). The last hope implicit in "Vivran costor?" (225; Shall they live?) is denied, and Macbeth must face the implacable reality of his own powerlessness. The realization is more than his mind can endure, and, as he faints, his crumpled body amidst the witches' supernatural cavorting provides a striking visual image of the mortal bounds that Macbeth could never escape.[15]

Verdi's decision to bring Lady Macbeth back for the end of the act is a dramatic anomaly, despite his assertion, "Non mi pare illogico che Lady, sempre intenta a sorvegliare il marito, abbia scoperto ove egli sia" (It does not seem illogical to me that Lady Macbeth, always intent on watching her husband, has discovered where he is).[16] Yet, at the same time, it also provides a subtle insight into Macbeth's changed state of being. The fire within him is extinguished, and his familiar words of domination and power now have a hollow ring. For the first time in the opera, Lady Macbeth pushes her husband to murder. When Macbeth recounts the apparition of Banco's heirs, Lady Macbeth cries, "Morte, sterminio sull'iniqua razza" (236; Death and extermination for his wretched race). Macbeth, however, seems at last to recognize the futility of continuing his struggle against fate and displaces his frustration onto Macduff: "Sì, morte!.. di Macduffo arda la rôcca! Perano moglie e prole." (236; Yes, death! Burn the fortress of Macduff! His wife and children shall die.) Lady Macbeth tries to refocus on Banco, "Di Banco il figlio... si rinvenga, e muoia" (236; Banco's son shall be brought back and shall die); but Macbeth is evasive, responding only with a general call for *vendetta* against all enemies. The ensuing duet, "Ora di morte" (237; Hour of death), is a hymn of personal domination over a hostile world, yet the largely dissimilar vocal lines of Macbeth and his wife subtly highlight the growing schism between the two conspirators, as Lady Macbeth tenaciously clings to a Will to Power that her husband senses is ultimately futile.

It is not until the final act, however, that Macbeth fully understands the terrible cost of his hubris. As his followers desert him to join Malcolm and the approaching English army, Macbeth remains confident of victory. His great *scena* is introduced with *fortissimo* brass in a statement of defiance that is carried through his declamatory recitative, "Perfidi! All'Anglo contro me v'unite" (275; Traitors! You join with the English against me). The upcoming battle will be the final test of his hold on the crown, but Macbeth has no doubts: "No, non temo di voi, nè del fanciullo che vi conduce" (276; No, I do not fear you, or the boy who leads you). Yet, he also realizes that he will win only a Pyrrhic victory. His Will to Power has secured him the crown but, in the process, has negated the sources of meaning in his life. Bombast thus gives way to the haunting whisper of "Eppur la vita sento nelle mie fibre inaridita" (276; And yet in the fiber of my being I feel my life has dried up), a *fil di voce* rising to a suspended D-flat in a subconscious echo of Macbeth's prescient recognition after the murder of Duncan, "Tutto è finito" (59; All is finished).

For Shakespeare's Macbeth, the final horror of his existence is the slow death of his soul, his ultimate inability to feel horror at all. Verdi's Macbeth, in contrast, is condemned to feel, to endure the torment of a life he created but no longer has the power to change. It is this agony of feeling that makes Macbeth's *cantabile* "Pietà, rispetto, amore" an almost unbearable expression of human suffering and loss (277; Compassion, respect, love, the comfort of declining years). Drawing on Shakespeare's "that which should accompany old age,/ As honor, love, obedience, troops of friends,/ I must not look to have; but in their stead,/ Curses, not loud but deep" (V.iii.24-27), Verdi adds the emotional resonance of a haunting melodic line that embodies Macbeth's "memory of what might have been."[17] A life of power without compassion and love is ultimately absurd, and it is poignantly ironic that only now, as Macbeth thinks of the life that has slipped away, does his usual dramatic declamation yield to the beauty of exquisitely expansive melody.

Macbeth has "liv'd long enough" (V.iii.22), and as he thinks of the curses that will follow him to his grave, his vocal line leaps an octave to a sustained, *tutta forza* E-flat on "ah! sol la bestemmia" (278; only curses). The graceful triplets that adorned the original melody are now transformed into the sobbing cries of mounting despair, as the vocal line *crescendos* to an anguished, *con forza* top F. At last, as the strings and woodwinds assume the melody, his thoughts drift, like autumn leaves carried by the current, toward a final void of utter alienation and devastation.

There is a nihilistic abandon in Macbeth's response to his wife's death, "La vita!.. che importa?" (281; Life! what does it matter?). Macbeth will play out the remainder of the charade that his life has become, but his Will to Power is destroyed. While operatic tradition would have called for a rousing *cabaletta* at the moment when his soldiers announce that Birnam Wood is coming against him, Macbeth gives voice only to a perfunctory series of unaccompanied cries: "Prodi all'armi!" (283; Brave ones, to arms!). His defiance is an empty gesture. When Macbeth is seen during the final battle, the stage directions note "Entra in iscena Macbeth incalzato da Macduff" (287; Macbeth enters, pursued by Macduff). Rather than trying to destroy his enemy, Macbeth warns, "Fuggi! nato di donna uccidermi non può" (287; Begone! none born of woman can kill me); even before the last disillusionment of

Macduff's "Nato non sono" (287; I was not born), Macbeth is a
broken man.

Drawing on the conclusion of Rusconi's Italian translation
of Shakespeare—which recalls the moralizing interpolations
of David Garrick on the eighteenth-century English stage—
the opera originally ended with Macbeth's final melodramatic
lament of damnation through ambition, "Vil corona" (Vile
crown). By 1865, however, Verdi found new dramatic power
in "poche parole" (few words). In a single "Cielo!" (288;
Heaven!), he concentrates the very essence of tragic anagnorisis, transforming a cliché into a compelling reaffirmation of
humanity's place in a larger cosmic order. Macbeth has tried to
defy the constraints of his own mortality, and his hubris has
brought him only inner torment and despair. Yet, his suffering
has led to a new understanding of the destruction wrought by
the siren call of the Superman, to a new recognition of the
transcendent hope offered by the regenerative bonds of compassion and love. Macbeth discovers the essence of his own
humanity and, in embracing both the glory and the limitations
of human existence, ascends to the heights of tragic heroism.

Rigoletto

Although Victor Hugo's plays inspired numerous operatic adaptations, none surpasses the dramatic power of *Rigoletto* (1851). In part, the success of the opera is due to the concision of plot, intensity of emotion, and compelling exploration of character that make Hugo's *Le Roi s'amuse* particularly suited to operatic performance. In a letter to his librettist Piave, Verdi recognized the potential of the play: "Tentate! il sogetto è grande, immenso, ed avvi un carattere che è una delle più grandi creazioni che vanti il teatro di tutti i paesi e di tutte le epoche. Il sogetto è *Le Roi s'amuse*, ed il carattere di cui ti parlo sarebbe Tribolet [*sic*]." (Give it a try! The subject is great, immense, and has a character that is one of the greatest creations that the theatre of all countries and times can boast. The subject is *Le Roi s'amuse,* and the character of which I speak is Triboulet.)[1] Hugo's court jester offered Verdi a "creazione degna di Shakespeare" (creation worthy of Shakespeare),[2] and he responded with a dramatic characterization that ranks as one of the greatest ever created for operatic baritone.[3]

Verdi insisted in a letter to La Fenice's Marzari that any bowdlerization of Hugo's play would subvert the dramatic truth of the opera: "Io trovo appunto bellissimo rappresentare questo personaggio esternamente difforme e ridicolo, ed internamente appassionato e pieno d'amore. Scelsi appunto tale sogetto per tutte queste qualità e questi tratti originali, se si tolgono io non posso più farvi musica. Se mi si dirà che le note possono stare egualmente su questo dramma, io rispondo che non comprendo queste ragioni, e dico francamente che le mie note o belle o brutte che siano non le scrivo a caso, e che procuro sempre di darle un carattere." (I find particularly beautiful the representation of this character, externally deformed and ridiculous and internally impassioned and full of love. I chose precisely such a subject for all these qualities and features, and if they are removed I cannot write the music. If you tell me that the notes can serve equally for this altered drama, I respond that I do not understand such judgments, and I say frankly that I do not write my music, whether beautiful or ugly, at random but always try to give it a specific dramatic character.)[4]

As a result of this insistence on fidelity to Hugo's drama, Piave's libretto for *Rigoletto* avoids the clichés and anomalies that mar many adaptations. Piave faithfully adheres to *Le Roi s'amuse* and succeeds in heightening the dramatic intensity of the original play through judicious compression. He focuses the libretto on the characters' psychological development and emotional bonds rather than on the social and political dynamics of Hugo's story. Ultimately, however, the libretto can only provide a dramatic framework for the composer's musical characterizations, and it is the power and insight of Verdi's portrayals that give *Rigoletto* an emotional resonance which surpasses Hugo's play. Verdi's scoring of *Rigoletto* is an innovative and strikingly effective example of *dramma per musica*—the form of musical expression developing organically out of the dramatic action, the flexible and nuanced scoring revealing, moment by moment, the nexus of thoughts, responses, and ambiguities that defines each character.

One nineteenth-century reviewer noted of *Le Roi s'amuse*, "C'est au coeur humain lui-même qu'il faut nous adresser pour déterminer la valeur de cette oeuvre nouvelle" (It is to the human heart itself that we must address ourselves to determine the worth of this new work).[5] The same is true for the compelling revelation of human struggle in Verdi's opera. Rigoletto is both a jester and a father, but he has tried to keep these two parts of his existence discrete. With the curse of Monterone, however, this division collapses, and Rigoletto is compelled to confront his own identity and the values by which he lives. He is a man whose very depth of feeling makes him vulnerable to a world of cruelty, betrayal, and loss. He is a man whose bitter defiance of the dehumanizing contempt of the court, whose desperate attempts to affirm his own humanity and to assert his worth as an individual, whose poignant need for love and compassion to redeem his life of misery reverberate not just in the mind but in the heart.

In *Le Roi s'amuse*, the jester Triboulet acts as a catalyst for events throughout the first act. He is not only a victim of his society but also an active participant in the process of corruption. He scoffs at the king's thoughts of bringing knowledge and art to his court: "Les femmes, Sire! ah Dieu! c'est le ciel, c'est la terre!/ C'est tout! Mais vous avez les femmes! vous avez/ Les femmes! laissez-moi tranquille! vous rêvez,/ De vouloir des savants." (Women, Sire! o God! that is Heaven and Earth! That is everything! Why, you have women, you have women! Nonsense! you are dreaming to want scholars.)[6] He cultivates animosity between the king and the nobles, telling François, "Sire, ils vous disent avare,/ Et qu'argent et faveurs s'en vont dans la Navarre," and adding maliciously, "Faites-les pendre" (1359-60; They say you are miserly and that money and favors vanish into Navarre . . . hang them).

Piave softens this view in his depiction of Rigoletto, for his jester merely responds to the Duke's desires rather than helping to form them. Rigoletto is not even present for the Duke's "Questa o quella" (This one or that one),[7] and when he does appear it is into a court that has already tacitly accepted the Duke's corrupt vision of life. Yet, when Rigoletto proposes the execution of Ceprano, he reveals a hatred that carries him beyond the bounds of sycophantic obeisance. For a moment the melody of the *banda* fades, and Rigoletto's musical line assumes dominance. There is a dark undercurrent in this rising phrase, with its fragmentation and aggressive use of monotone repetition, as the jester declares, "Che far di tal testa?.. A cosa ella vale?" (29-30; What is to be done with such a head?.. What is the use of it?).

In the following ensemble, where the Duke reprimands Rigoletto and the courtiers vow vengeance, Verdi transforms a moment of potential dramatic stasis into an insightful exploration of psychology. Although the Duke repeats five times, "Ah sempre tu spingi lo scherzo all'estremo" (31-32; You always push the joke to the extreme), there is more laughter than stern reproach in his fragmented vocal line: the Duke cares little for the courtiers, and he cares no more for Rigoletto. Thus, having laid full responsibility for the courtiers' hatred on the jester, the Duke returns to his own pleasures with the cry "Tutto è gioia" (44; All is joy). Rigoletto is deluded in believing that the Duke will really protect him, for self-gratification is the Duke's only concern.

Like the Duke, Rigoletto denies the implications of his actions, treating the world of the court as a self-contained sphere in which his hatred and revenge may be unleashed with impunity. In attacking Monterone, however, he inadvertently blurs his carefully maintained division between Rigoletto the jester and Rigoletto the father. Piave portrays Monterone as an archetypal parent, deleting the political details and the rejection of his dishonored daughter that color Hugo's original portrait of M. de Saint-Vallier. Further, Rigoletto mocks Monterone not as a courtier but as a father, jeeringly transforming Monterone's vocal line into a travesty of dignity and righteous indignation: "Voi congiuraste, voi congiuraste contro noi, Signore, e noi, e noi, clementi in vero, perdonammo... Qual vi piglia or delirio... a tutte l'ore di vostra figlia a reclamar l'onore?" (51-52; You conspired against us, sir; and we, truly merciful, pardoned you. What delirium now seizes you that you protest at all hours the honor of your daughter?) The middle C's on "congiuraste" and "noi" are stretched to ludicrous length only to be undercut by comically pompous orchestral interjections, while sarcastic trills on "delirio" and "l'onore" complete Rigoletto's scornful parody.

Rigoletto attacks a father, and it is a father's curse that Monterone hurls at his tormentor: "Slanciare il cane al leon morente è vile, o Duca... [*a Rigoletto*] e tu serpente, tu che d'un padre ridi al dolore, sii maledetto" (57; To set a dog upon a dying lion is vile, o Duke... [to Rigoletto] and you, serpent, who laugh at a father's sorrow, be cursed). Unlike Hugo's original scene, in which M. de Saint-Vallier focuses as much on François as on Triboulet, the weight of Monterone's curse falls entirely on Rigoletto in a seven-fold repetition of "sii maledetto." This malediction is responsible for a blinding moment of self-knowledge, as Rigoletto suddenly realizes the horrors in which he is implicated. It is the man and the father, not the court jester, who gasps throughout the ensemble that concludes the scene, "Che sento! orrore" (57-58; What do I hear! Horror).[8]

In his justifying preface to *Le Roi s'amuse*, published after the play was banned, Hugo suggests that the "sujet véritable du drame, c'est la *malédiction de M. de Saint-Vallier*" (The true subject of the drama is the *curse of M. de Saint-Vallier*).[9] Yet, in both the play and the opera, it is clear that the curse functions more as a catalyst for the jester's self-discovery than for the subsequent events of the plot.[10] As Rigoletto returns to his secluded home, he evidences a nascent self-awareness. In his thoughts of killing the Duke, there is an ill-defined desire to atone for the evil he has perpetrated in his role as jester; although he does not engage the services of the assassin Sparafucile, he asks, "E quanto spendere per un Signor dovrei?" (77-78; And how much would I have to spend for a gentleman?).

Rigoletto is not driven to act at this time because he still believes that he can keep the two spheres of his existence separate, but the collapse of this dichotomy has already begun. In the dramatic recitative "Pari siamo" following Sparafucile's departure, Rigoletto looks into his own soul. There is a poignant sense of loneliness and isolation in the unaccompanied phrases with which he recognizes his degradation. His torment is evident in the breathless fragmentation and propulsive dotted rhythms of his rising vocal line: "Pari siamo!.. io la lingua, egli ha il pugnale!.. l'uomo son io che ride, ei quel che spegne" (83; We are equals! I have my tongue, he the dagger! I am the man who laughs, he the one who kills). A punctuating series of string figures suggests Rigoletto's stream of consciousness as his thoughts return to a haunted, *morendo* echo of Monterone's curse, "Quel vecchio maledivami" (83; That old man cursed me).

As Rigoletto recognizes what he has become, his bitterness explodes in a lunging *allegro* vocal line heightened by string underscoring: "O uomini!.. o natura!.. vil scellerato mi faceste voi" (84; O mankind! o nature! you made me vile and wretched). The frustration and almost unbearable rage he feels at the dehumanizing environment in which he is trapped explodes in the violent, rising attacks and agitated orchestration of "Oh rabbia!.. esser difforme! oh rabbia!.. esser buffone! Non dover, non poter altro che ridere." (84-85; O rage, to be deformed! o rage, to be a buffoon! No duty, no power other than to laugh.) To the court, Rigoletto is not a man, but a hunchback and a jester. Yet, as Triboulet cries, "Ô pauvre fou de cour!—C'est un homme, après tout" (1380; Poor jester!—He is a man, after all). His essential humanity is denied, and it is this loss that finds expression in the mournful adagio lament, where the vocal line is softened by legato phrasing and the infinite longing in a suspended D: "Il retaggio d'ogn'uom m'è tolto... il pianto" (85; Tears, the property of every man, are denied me).

Like Triboulet, Rigoletto engages in acts of cruelty and hatred not merely because of his deformity or occupation, but in reaction to the contempt and degradation with which he is treated.[11] Stripped of his own humanity by the court, Rigoletto tries to dehumanize his persecutors. Yet, embracing the corruption of the world around him in this spirit of negation brings him only more bitterness and inner suffering. Significantly, Rigoletto culminates his statement of hatred not with the ostensible joy of "Quanta in mordervi ho gioia" (What joy I have in stinging you), but with the tormented, *tutta forza* recognition of degradation, "Se iniquo son, per cagion vostra è solo" (86; If I am wicked it is only due to you).

Rigoletto still clings to the belief that his public world of torment can be kept apart from his private world of parental love. Embodied in the delicate melody of a solo flute, the pure serenity of love displaces the rage that has engulfed him, and Rigoletto echoes this caressing melodic phrase as he asserts the fundamental duality within himself: "Ma in altr'uomo qui mi cangio" (86-87; But here I am changed into another man). Yet once again, Rigoletto's mind returns to the horror of "Quel vecchio maledivami" (87); Monterone's curse has already brought about a subconscious realization that the dichotomy between jester and father is insupportable. There is thus a poignant desperation in Rigoletto's willful effort to deny his own doubts and fears, the defiance of "è follia" (87-88; It is folly) pointedly subverted by a virtually unaccompanied vocal line that rises only to a strangely unconvincing top E.

Rigoletto succeeds, at least momentarily, in banishing the outside world from his thoughts as he greets his daughter with an emotionally expansive *allegro brillante*: "Mia vita sei! Senza te in terra qual bene avrei?" (89; You are my life! Without you, what love would I have on earth?) However, Gilda senses an undercurrent of sadness and begins to probe into the mysteries of her father's past. As Rigoletto tells Gilda of her mother, he reveals a haunting insight into the man he might have become. Only his wife could see Rigoletto as a man rather than a hunchback, and her love had the power to redeem the hatred and scorn of an entire world.

The narrow range of his *pianissimo andante* line reveals the great strain Rigoletto endures in maintaining some degree of emotional control as he whispers, "Deh non parlare al misero del suo perduto bene" (92-93; Ah, do not speak to the wretched man of his lost love). In confronting the pain of his loss, in baring his soul to Gilda, in revealing to her the vulnerable heart that beats beneath the cynical façade he displays in public, Rigoletto makes the ultimate gesture of love to his daughter. He speaks of the understanding and compassion that his wife offered him: "Ella sentia, quell' angelo, pietà delle mie pene" (93; She felt, that angel, pity for my sufferings). A single grace note enriches his established melody in a telling indication of heightened feeling that culminates in a *crescendo* of rising eighth notes before a caressing final *diminuendo*.

El - la   sen-tia.   quel - l'an - ge-lo.   pie - tà   del - le   mie   pe - ne...

The anguish with which Rigoletto recalls how once his degradation was transformed through the power of love is clear as his fragmented vocal line builds to a *dolce* E-flat on "Solo, difforme, povero, per compassion mi amò" (93; Alone, deformed, poor, in her compassion she loved me). There is almost unspeakable desolation in his climactic "Ah morìa" (93; She died), a cry of agony that surges from an unaccompanied, extended E-flat to F-flat before the vocal line collapses. As Rigoletto reinternalizes his grief, his *piangendo* repetition of "morìa" finds expression in a stifled musical phrase that falls only a half step from B-double flat to A-flat. Yet, out of Rigoletto's sorrow comes joy for the gift of his daughter; and the emotional enervation of his monotone, triple *pianissimo* "Sola or tu resti, sola or tu resti al misero" gives way to the expansiveness of "Dio, sii ringraziato, sii ringraziato!" (93-94; Only you now remain, only you now remain to this wretched man—God, be thanked!).

Eventually, Gilda is able to dry his tears, and Rigoletto joins
in her animated vocal line. But his daughter cannot offer him
the undivided love he received from his wife. Gilda has her own
life, and her romantic feelings for the Duke are ultimately
stronger than her devotion to her father. Rigoletto wants to
make Gilda his entire world, as he cries, "Culto, famiglia, patria,
il mio universo, il mio universo è in te" (100; Religion, family,
homeland, my universe, my universe is in you). Marked *con effu-
sione*, Rigoletto's building vocal line, with its lunging phrases and
powerfully even rhythms, conveys the intensity of his vision.
Gilda responds with devotion, but not with an identical vision,
as she declares, "Ah se può lieto rendervi, gioia è la vita, la vita
a me" (100-101; If I can make you happy, my life is joy to me).
Although her vocal line echoes Rigoletto's melody at times, it
also retains its individual identity. Even more significantly,
Gilda immediately returns to her thoughts of the outside world,
as she asks her father for permission to see the city.

While Gilda provides the only source of meaning in
Rigoletto's life, his relationship with her is colored by the

inescapable miasma of the court. The Edenic isolation of his enclosed garden cannot be maintained, and Rigoletto's peace is marred by intrusive doubts and suspicions. Even his farewell to his daughter is framed in terms of an admonition to her duenna: "veglia, o donna, questo fiore che a te puro confidai" (105; O woman, watch over this pure flower that I entrusted to you). Ironically, when Rigoletto interrupts his reprise of this melody to investigate a noise outside the garden, he unknowingly allows the Duke to slip into the sanctuary; his final repetition of "veglia, o donna" is already too late.

Gilda distances herself from her father's concerns, reiterating her faith in Heaven with a light *staccato* line that seems to anticipate the dreamy idealism of her vision of love in "Caro nome" (140; Dear name). The romantic idealism in Gilda's fantasy of the Duke is juxtaposed with the decadent reality of the outside world as the courtiers gather in the street for the kidnapping. In a moment of supreme irony, Rigoletto's delusion that his private life can be sheltered from corruption is shattered: the jester unwittingly conspires in his own daughter's abduction while eagerly helping the courtiers with their fictitious scheme to seize the Countess Ceprano. His metaphoric blindness in thinking he is protecting Gilda is signaled by the blindfold he wears while holding the ladder for the courtiers' escapade.

When Rigoletto awakens to the horror of his own actions, his grief and despair surpass his capacity for articulate expression. Searching in vain for his beloved daughter, he is a man on the verge of complete mental collapse, wanting to scream but trapped in a nightmare world which deprives him of all sound. With almost superhuman effort he gives voice to the single cry that encompasses a lifetime of misery, degradation, and loss:

"Ah! ah! ah!.. la maledizione!" (176; Ah, the curse!). In this context, Rigoletto's loss of consciousness at the end of the act is no mere theatrical *coup*, but a dramatic insight into a mind that cannot endure such an intensity of pain and still cling to sanity.

The Duke's affected sentimentality and underlying indifference to Gilda's abduction at the opening of the second act provide a powerful dramatic foil for the internalized agony of Rigoletto as he enters the court in search of his daughter. In Hugo's scene, Triboulet joins in a song with the courtiers, but Verdi provides a more telling insight as Rigoletto, *affettando indifferenza*, sings a melody on the nonsense syllables "La ra" (225). He struggles to keep the vocal line raised in a show of carefree ease, but the melody continually sinks again in an understated indication of the jester's enormous emotional strain.[12]

It is not until he discovers that Gilda is with the Duke that Rigoletto abandons his charade, erupting *con accento terribile* into a wrenching, *fortissimo*, "Io vo' mia figlia" (238; I want my daughter). Rigoletto's following denunciation of his tormentors combines an emotionally frenzied orchestration with a furiously declamatory vocal line: "Cortigiani, vil razza dannata, per qual prezzo vendeste il mio bene?" (240; Courtiers—vile, damned race—for what price did you sell my happiness?) Piave eliminates the extended personal attacks that Hugo's Triboulet launches against the courtiers: "Vos mères aux laquais se sont prostituées!/ Vous êtes tous bâtards." (1429; Your mothers prostituted themselves with lackeys! You are all bastards.) The result is to heighten the nobility of a father trying in vain to defend his child against a corrupt world. Significantly, the descending pattern of Rigoletto's first assault is abruptly reversed, the vocal line rising to a thunderous repetition of

E-flat, as the father tries to negate the degradation of the court with the purity of his daughter: "ma mia figlia è impagabil tesor" (240-41; but my daughter is a priceless treasure).

As a father Rigoletto finds the strength to challenge the court, crying, "nulla interra più l'uomo paventa, se de' figli difende l'onor" (241-42; a man no longer fears anything on earth if he is defending the honor of his children). A menacing series of middle C's *crescendo* to a *forte* E-flat on "paventa" in an expression of courage that culminates in the repeated E-flats of "difende." In this context the traditionally interpolated high G's on "difende l'onor" are psychologically revealing, emphasizing the act of will by which Rigoletto tries to assert his control over the court. Yet, this attempt at self-affirmation is ultimately futile, and, as he is physically overwhelmed by the courtiers, Rigoletto seems a broken man.

Casting aside the defenses with which he tried to protect himself from their cruelty and abuse, Rigoletto reaches out to the courtiers for human pity and understanding in a sobbing, disjointed *meno mosso*: "Ah! Ebben, piango... Marullo... Signore, tu ch'hai l'alma gentil come il core" (243; Ah then I weep...

Marullo... Lord... you who have a soul as gentle as your heart).
As Rigoletto begs Marullo for an answer, there is a pitiable
eagerness in his fragmented triplet phrases; and when the futility of his pleas becomes apparent, his despair is captured in a
collapsing vocal line and the utter desolation of a final octave
leap to a fading F on the words "tu taci" (244; You are silent).

Finally, with an intensity of suffering that negates his own
past corruption, Rigoletto pleads for pity from a pitiless world.
His depth of feeling is highlighted by the swelling phrases and
sobbing grace notes of the vocal line, as he reveals his own vulnerability, begging his tormentors for forgiveness: "Miei
Signori... perdono, pietate... al vegliardo la figlia ridate"
(244-45; My lords... forgive me, have pity... give an old man
back his daughter). Repeating "Signori, perdon, perdono,
pietà" (245-46), he can barely give voice to a suffocated series
of *pianissimo* sobs. Rigoletto is humiliated, debased, crushed by
the enemies he so long held at bay, and his love for the daughter who alone brings meaning to his life is powerfully
expressed in the leaping, *con forza* cry, "ridate a me la figlia"
(246; Give me back my daughter). The vocal line jumps a sixth
to a pair of keening musical phrases, gaining even greater emotional intensity on the second repetition of Rigoletto's plea
with a full octave leap on "ridate" and a surging, climactic high
G-flat on the key word "me" before a despairing descent. His
final "pietà," however, is met only with silence in the extended
rest that concludes the aria (246); and the brief moment of joy
when Gilda rushes to his arms is crushed by the realization of
his daughter's defilement.

Gilda's degradation turns Rigoletto's life of suffering and
torment into unredeemed, meaningless absurdity: "Solo per me
l'infamia a te chiedeva, o Dio! ch'ella potesse ascendere quanto

caduto er'io" (255-56; O God, I asked that infamy be mine alone, that she might rise as far as I had fallen). Ironically echoing Monterone's vocal line, Rigoletto begins with a numbed repetition of middle C, but his desolation over the loss of the only remaining purity and innocence in his existence cannot be contained in so narrow a musical line. His vocal phrases surge first to D-flat on "infamia" and then to a more-extended E-flat on "Dio," before climaxing in an expansive return to E-flat on "ascendere."

Rigoletto grieves as a father, and it is also as a father that he comforts Gilda. His is the voice of unwavering love expressed in tenderly arching, *pianissimo* phrases heightened by mournful orchestral doubling on "piangi, piangi, fanciulla" (257; Weep, weep, child).

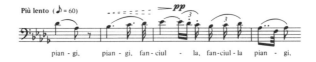

Rigoletto and his daughter are driven apart again at the end of the act by his determination to destroy the Duke. Seeing Monterone on his way to prison, Rigoletto takes upon himself the role of paternal avenger: "Sì, vendetta, tremenda vendetta di quest'anima è solo desio" (265; Yes, vengeance, terrible vengeance is my soul's only desire). Rigoletto intends to kill the Duke as a final affirmation of divine justice; but in arrogating to himself such responsibility, he commits an ultimately catastrophic act of hubris: "Come fulmin scagliato da Dio te colpire il buffone saprà" (266-67; Like a thunderbolt hurled by

God, the buffoon will strike you). There is the rush of retribution, but also a hint of savage personal triumph in the headlong pace of Rigoletto's *allegro vivo*, with its powerful combination of hammering dotted half notes and vigorous triplets.

Verdi infuses the traditional *cabaletta* form with the dramatic vitality of a *scena* as Gilda pleads with mounting anxiety for the life of her lover.[13] Her vocal line repeats Rigoletto's original melody, now raised a fourth as she vainly urges forgiveness. There is no reconciliation of Rigoletto's determination for vengeance and Gilda's pleas for mercy; hence, even in the closing *stretta*, the two vocal lines fail to join in standard unison declamation. The traditional interpolations at the end of the duet crystalize the dramatic situation, for Gilda's desperate high E-flat is ultimately overwhelmed by the furious strength of Rigoletto's high A-flat.

Despite his apparent intransigence and disregard for Gilda's entreaties, Rigoletto does not immediately proceed with his planned vengeance. At the opening of the third act, it is clear that he does not view his revenge as simply a parental prerogative. He wants his daughter's assent to his action, and in order to dispel her belief that the Duke still loves her, he brings Gilda to witness the Duke seducing Sparafucile's sister, Maddalena.

In *Le Roi s'amuse*, Blanche responds to her lover's betrayal by acceding at last to her father's desire for revenge: "Hélas!— Faites/ Tout ce que vous voudrez" (1448; Alas! Do what you wish). Gilda gives no such explicit sanction, but Rigoletto believes he has her tacit approval before he sends her off to Verona. There is an oppressive irony in his plans to preserve his child while he remains to contract the Duke's murder, for it is still impossible for Rigoletto to distance Gilda from the repercussions of his hatred and revenge.

In the heightened emotional power of its final scenes, *Rigoletto* departs most significantly from *Le Roi s'amuse*. The hubris in the savage joy Triboulet exhibits when he returns to claim the body of his victim is mitigated by the compression of the opera libretto and Verdi's understated recitative. Though the vocal line rises to a sustained F on "oh gioia," the lack of melodic scope in the recitative undercuts the malevolence of Rigoletto's "Quest'è un buffone, ed un potente è questo!.. Ei sta sotto i miei piedi!.. È desso! oh gioia." (342-43; This is a buffoon, and a mighty man is this one! He is under my feet! It is he! oh joy.) It is as if in his moment of presumptive victory and complete self-affirmation, there is a part of Rigoletto that subconsciously recognizes the futility of his vengeance. Killing the Duke cannot redeem a corrupt world, and hence Rigoletto's act of vengeance ends on a rather anticlimactic, static repetition of D-sharp for "All'onda! all'onda" (343-44; Into the waves). The impotence of this action is immediately highlighted: the oblivious Duke passes upstage singing a reprise of "La donna è mobile" (344; Woman is fickle), while Rigoletto discovers the body of his dying daughter. The Duke is invulnerable because, in his complete self-absorption, he is indifferent to cruelty, betrayal, and loss; but Gilda and Rigoletto are destroyed because they both feel too deeply.

Through the purity of her faith in love and forgiveness, Gilda is able to transfigure even death itself.[14] There is a serene ascendence in her delicately suspended, *pianissimo* vision of Heaven: "Lassù in cielo, vicino alla madre... in eterno per voi pregherò" (352-53; Up there in Heaven, near to my mother... I will pray for you forever). But this vision only emphasizes the

Hell into which Rigoletto has been irretrievably cast. As he tries to cling to the one human being who could save him from bitterness and despair, he is a man adrift. In contrast to the serene confidence of Gilda's vocal line is the surging grief of Rigoletto's "Non morir... mio tesoro pietade" (353; Do not die... my treasure... pity) and the inescapable desolation of "Se t'involi... qui sol, qui sol rimarrei... non morire... o qui teco morrò" (354-55; If you fly away... alone, alone here I would remain... Do not die... or I will die here with you).

An unbridgeable divide now separates father and daughter, and there is no need for Hugo's ill-conceived chorus of unfeeling townspeople to point out Rigoletto's absolute and horrible isolation. His desperate efforts at self-affirmation are transmuted into devastating self-negation with the death of Gilda. Rigoletto is condemned to life after the only source of meaning in that life is gone, and his terrible recognition of ultimate human vulnerability is captured in the unbearable anguish of his final rending cry, "Ah! la maledizione" (357).[15]

La Traviata

*L*a Traviata (1853) is a classic illustration of opera's capacity to create dramatic characterizations that transcend the original source play in complexity and human insight. Georges Duval, little more than an implacable melodramatic villain in *La Dame aux camélias* by Alexandre Dumas fils, is transformed into the character of Giorgio Germont, a man trying to reconcile his inner being with the public persona his bourgeois status compels him to adopt. Rather than merely following Dumas' portrayal and depicting Germont as a "moralist who stands for and speaks for the values of bourgeois respectability,"[1] Verdi and his librettist Piave developed a tautly dramatic characterization that illuminates one human being's personal growth, struggle for self-realization, and psychological metamorphosis. Dumas' simple embodiment of destructive bourgeois self-righteousness is transformed into a hauntingly prescient image of the modern individual's search for personal identity in the face of the suffocating society in which he is trapped.

The characterization of Germont goes beyond melodramatic stereotype and cliché to explore the struggle, torment, and ultimate loss of a man compelled to play a social role fundamentally antithetical to his human nature. As the reviewer for the *Illustrated London News* insightfully noted of one nineteenth-century performance: "The struggle between the old man's sense of inexorable duty and his kindly and compassionate nature is drawn with true pathos."[2] Unlike Duval, Germont is a pawn in a game of social mores over which he has no control. His confrontation with Violetta is not the result of his own inner imperative, but of external coercion. Germont himself is a hapless performer, trying to fulfill the role of "Father" dictated by the society of Provence, trying to preserve his daughter's happiness by bowing to the wishes of her fiancé's family. Yet, during his wrenching scene with Violetta, Germont increasingly finds his social mask insupportable. He begins to reevaluate his way of life, and this process inevitably moves him not only toward a new understanding of conduct and personal relationships but also toward an abandonment of many bourgeois values by which he has lived.[3]

To accommodate the dramatic and psychological scope of the pivotal second act dialogue between Germont and Violetta, Verdi creates a ground-breaking *scena* that incorporates elements of traditional recitative, aria, and duet forms into a uni-

fied scoring. The *allegro* strings that announce the entrance of
Germont immediately presage both the banality and the ponderous pretension of the bourgeois image he projects, but in
the interplay of his words and music Germont evidences his
unease with this role. He hurtles through his business like a
man reciting a script he is afraid of forgetting. Gone are the
civilities and conversation in Dumas' play, as Germont
unleashes a torrent of self-righteous indignation: "Madamigella
Valery?.. D'Alfredo il padre in me vedete. Sì, dell'incauto, che a
ruina corre, ammaliato da voi." (Mademoiselle Valery? You see
in me the father of Alfredo. Yes, of the rash boy who runs to his
ruin, bewitched by you.)[4] Yet, Verdi's recitative emphasizes the
exaggerated and forced tone of this denunciation. Germont's
contemptuous "Madamigella Valery" explodes on a jarring
interval, up a fourth instead of the anticipated third from the
orchestral introduction. Germont is pushing too hard, barely
pausing long enough for Violetta's responses. Verdi accentuates
the momentum in these lines with a pounding use of monotone
repetition in a vocal part that rises with calculated ferocity to
top each of Violetta's interjections with the leap of a third. At
the same time, however, beginning each of Germont's phrases
on the offbeat of the measure subtly suggests the slight hesita-
tion of an imperfectly memorized performance. Germont is
playing a part, though like an inexperienced performer, he
overacts.

Violetta's dignified "Donna son io, signore, ed in mia casa"
(91; I am a woman, sir, and in my own house) is a clear departure from the scenario Germont prepared in Provence, and his
bellicose rhetoric soon disintegrates into inarticulate confusion:
"(Quai modi!) Pure..." (92; [What manners!] Yet...). In Dumas'
play, by contrast, Duval responds to Marguerite with unyield-

ing cynicism, "En vérité, quand on entend ce langage, quand on voit ces façons, on a peine à se dire que ce langage est d'emprunt, que ces façons sont acquises. On me l'avait bien dit, que vous étiez une dangereuse personne." (In truth, hearing this language and seeing these manners, it is difficult to tell oneself that the language is borrowed and the manners are acquired. They were right to tell me that you are a dangerous person.)[5] While Duval confronts Marguerite because of personal conviction, Germont does not, and his vocal line becomes fragmented by uncertainty as he attempts to return to his script.

The revelation that Violetta has sold her belongings to pay the debts of this idyllic retreat shatters what remains of the stereotypic image of the demi-mondaine Germont has been led to expect. As a human being, rather than a spokesman for bourgeois morality, he is already coming to recognize the cruel myopia of the values of Provence. Significantly, while Duval offers only a formal and perfunctory apology for thinking Marguerite mercenary, Germont gives voice to a lament that captures the inescapable tension between his nascent awareness and the action that his bourgeois society nonetheless compels him to take: "Ah il passato perchè, perchè v'accusa?" (92-93; Ah the past, why does it accuse you?). This poignant fragment provides the first real glimpse of the man beneath the mask, and at this point Verdi introduces Germont's first melodic phrase in the scene, creating an emotionally weighted moment that suggests his sorrow and helplessness in the face of implacable society.

After the expansive outpouring of Violetta's "Più non esiste" (93; It exists no longer), Germont tries to regain the self-control he needs to fulfill his assignment. There is still a hint of sadness in his admission, "Nobili sensi invero" (93;

Noble feelings indeed), but the vocal line is already taking on a
new sense of restraint as Germont moves toward his inevitable
conclusion, "Ed a tai sensi un sacrifizio chieggo" (93; and of
such feelings I ask a sacrifice). Just as he redirects Violetta's
nobility of spirit, so Germont fittingly appropriates and dis-
torts her melodic line, rising to a jarring E for "un sacrifizio"
before a hammering denouement.

It is a return to the harsh reality of social necessity, but
Germont already has enough respect for Violetta to admit his
real motivations rather than camouflage his intent behind
self-righteous accusations. Again he begins, "D'Alfredo il padre"
(94), but the phrase is imbued with a new sensibility: what at
the opening of the scene conveyed arrogance and intimidation
here suggests a subconscious effort to distance himself from his
terrible request. The fragmentation of the vocal line, with its
irregular rhythms and unpretentious conclusion, clearly reveals
a man struggling for words, casting aside his script and trying to
communicate with a new honesty of feeling and expression: "la
sorte, l'avvenir domanda or qui de'suoi due figli" (94; Alfredo's
father asks now for the fate, the future of his two children).

In *La Dame aux camélias* Duval claims to be motivated only
by his daughter's impending marriage, but his personal animosity and bitterness are apparent throughout the cold inter-
change with Marguerite and undermine any pretext that he is
acting from external pressure: "je l'avais écrit à Armand, mais
Armand, tout à vous, n'a pas même recu mes lettres; j'aurais pu
mourir sans qu'il le sût" (128; I wrote to Armand, but Armand,
belonging only to you, did not even receive my letters. I could
have died without his knowing). Duval may speak of the
demands of provincial society, but it is clear that the verdict of
that society is one he shares. He may speak of how purified

Marguerite is in his eyes, but he inevitably returns to a cutting assessment of her irredeemable dishonor: "Eh bien, ma fille, ma Blanche bien-aimée épouse un honnête homme; elle entre dans une famille honorable, qui veut que tout soit honorable dans la mienne" (128; Well, my daughter, my beloved Blanche is marrying a respectable man; she is entering a respectable family that wishes everything to be respectable in mine).

This underlying personal contempt is deleted in Piave's text, and Germont is personally untroubled by Alfredo's love. He agreed to confront Violetta only when threatened with the destruction of his daughter's happiness, and, as he confesses that societal coercion compelled him to come to Paris, Germont betrays a Romantic spirit beneath his austere façade. Casting aside conventional decorum, he opens his heart to Violetta; Germont's idealized vision of his daughter is not a cliché of bourgeois family values, but a nonjudgmental celebration of happiness and love that stands in stark contrast to Duval's contractual calculation.

The respect Germont feels for Violetta serves as a catalyst for his own personal growth as he tries to find a new form of expression to give voice to his paternal love. Verdi highlights the simple sincerity in Germont's words with a *dolcissimo cantabile*, uniting a tender, delicate vocal line with simple orchestration: "Pura siccome un angelo Iddio mi diè una figlia" (94; God gave to me a daughter pure as an angel; if Alfredo does not return to the bosom of his family. . .).[6] There is a certain hesitancy in the repetition of his initial two-measure phrase that suggests Germont's reticence at such an expression of emotion, but his confidence increases and the vocal line expands into a swelling *legato* phrase that captures his pain in facing the destruction of his daughter's dream of love.

Pu - ra siccome un an - gelo   Id - dio mi diè una   fi - glia;

se Al - fredo ne - ga   rie - dere in   se - no alla   fa - mi - glia.

Poetic effusion, however, is certainly not Germont's accus-
tomed form of expression, and Verdi's scoring highlights the
limitations Germont is trying to overcome. His vocal line cannot keep pace with the development of his thoughts and
returns to a reprise of his initial melody in the middle of a sentence: "l'amato e amante giovine, cui sposa andar dovea, or si
ricusa al vincolo che lieti, lieti ne rendeva" (95; the beloved
and loving young man whose bride she was going to be will
now refuse the bond that made them both so happy). There is
a heightened intensity in the *leggero* figures that ornament
"giovine" and "dovea," but the only release for this underlying
feeling comes in a rise to F, rather than the original D-flat, on
"vincolo." Indeed, the vocal melody immediately breaks down
into a series of urgently mounting, heavily fragmented phrases
for "Deh non mutate in triboli le rose dell'amor" (95).

At this moment, however, Germont seems to become
aware of the irony in his plea, and the vocal line returns to a
self-conscious repetition of monotone eighth notes. There is a
palpable sense of urgency in the plunging phrases with which
he brings his entreaty to a close, but it is coupled with a draining of melodic inspiration that emphasizes the awkwardness of
a man unsure of what step to take next (95-96; Ah, do not

change into tribulations the roses of love... your heart must not
resist my prayers, no, no).

In Dumas' play, Duval evidences no such hesitancy or
self-consciousness. He relentlessly presses Marguerite to leave
Armand, brushing aside her "Quitter Armand, monsieur, autant
me tuer tout de suite" (130; To leave Armand, sir, would be
equal to killing me immediately). To this end Duval creates a
calculated, minutely detailed picture of Marguerite's desolate
future of ostracism and despair, deprived of family, career,
beauty, and love. His monologue is a full-scale assault on
Marguerite's sensibilities, a merciless manipulation of her deep-
est fears. Throughout, Duval also maintains an ugly tone of
condescension and contempt. Beneath his empty phrases of
sympathy and understanding, Duval's bourgeois condemnation
is ever-present, culminating in the implication that Marguerite
has experienced all the happiness a woman of her kind has any
right to expect, and that by renouncing Armand she can at
least gain some degree of self-respect: "Vous avez été heureuse
trois mois, ne tachez pas ce bonheur dont la continuité est
impossible; gardez-en le souvenir dans votre coeur; qu'il vous
rende forte, c'est tout ce que vous avez le droit de lui deman-

der. Un jour, vous serez fière de ce que vous aurez fait, et, toute votre vie, vous aurez l'estime de vous-même." (132; You have been happy for three months, do not seek a joy the continuation of which is impossible; keep the memory of it in your heart; it will make you strong, and that is all you have the right to demand of it. One day you will be proud of what you have done, and all your life you will have your self-esteem.)

In contrast to Duval's pontificating, Germont struggles to justify the sacrifice he is asking, not only to Violetta but to himself. Verdi emphasizes the conscious effort by which Germont asserts his self-control after Violetta's near-hysterical "Non sapete" (97; You do not know). Studiously calming descending phrases, weighted with the added gravity of orchestral doubling, bring about a deliberate lessening of emotional intensity as Germont acknowledges, "È grave il sagrifizio; ma pur, tranquilla uditemi" (99-100; It is a heavy sacrifice, but listen to me calmly). Yet, the rests between these phrases, in addition to the *lunga pausa* before Germont is able to continue with his rationalization, reveal his inner struggle to regain his composure.

While Duval simply continues his diatribe, Germont seems to search for some appropriate response from a woefully inadequate repertoire of bourgeois platitudes. Violetta immediately rejects his first hesitant "Bella voi siete e giovine... col tempo..." (100; You are beautiful and young... with time...). His next tactic, however, strikes a more responsive chord. Underscored by an ominous *crescendo* in the orchestra, Germont touches on Violetta's unspoken fears: "ma volubile sovente è l'uom" (100-101; but man is often inconstant). He then knows what line of rationalization to pursue. Yet, in contrast to Duval's pointed cruelty, Germont's text for "Un dì" (101; One day) suggests, in its understatement, a real compassion, and a general reference to "il tedio" (101; tedium) replaces the extended vision of misery indulged in by Duval.

Verdi's scoring emphasizes the restraint in Germont's approach. A mechanical sequence of fragmented sixteenth notes and grinding thirty-second-note figures captures both the tedium Germont is describing and a metaphoric wearing down of Violetta's resistance. But the vocal line, marked *con semplicità* and *pianissimo*, eschews a melodramatically hectoring tone. Indeed, the dry detachment in this *andante piuttosto mosso*, the lack of true emotional weight even when the line finally *crescendos* to top F, subtly highlights his lack of conviction in the platitudes he is mouthing: "poichè dal ciel non furono... tai nodi benedetti" (101-102; because such bonds were not blessed from Heaven).

While Duval demands Marguerite's sacrifice as if it were his right, Germont begs it with the humility of prayer, imploring, "siate di mia famiglia... l'angel consolatore" (102; Be the consoling angel of my family). It is at this moment, when stock moralizing gives way to genuine personal appeal, that Germont's initial melody is transmuted. With heightened *legato* and swelling phrases, the vocal line captures Germont's new emotional involvement. As his inner voice presses against the constraints of his scripted verbal expression, the vocal line strains against the established rhythmic pattern in the developing syncopation of "famiglia... l'angel consolator."

sia - te di mia fa - mi - glia .... l'an - gel con - sola - tore...

Finally, as in "Pura siccome un angelo," the melody breaks down into a sequence of urgently rising, monotone phrases that suggest Germont's inability to find a form of expression which captures the intensity of his feelings. It is significant, however, that as Germont ends his plea he subconsciously distances himself, insisting with perhaps too much vigor that God, rather than social necessity, inspires his words. Further, he emphasizes that it is only in his role of father that he asks such a sacrifice; hence, the vocal line leaps a sixth to an emphatic F extended with a fermata on "genitor" for the conclusion of "è Dio che ispira tai detti a un genitor" (103; It is God who inspires such words from a father).

Despite his new understanding and sympathy, Germont cannot defy the dictates of Provence if he is to preserve the happiness of his own daughter. As he repeats his plea, Violetta recognizes society's inexorable hostility. Her desolate "Dite alla giovine" (105; Say to the young girl) forces Germont to face an agonizing image of human suffering. Piave elaborates Duval's perfunctory "Pauvre femme" (133; Poor woman) into an expansive expression of compassion, but it is Verdi's scoring that provides an even subtler illumination of character.

While ostensibly offering comfort to Violetta, Germont's vocal line is too agitated in its heightened *tessitura*, too weighted with orchestral doubling, too turbulent in its lunging phrases for simple solace. Instead, it reveals a soul in torment: "Piangi, piangi, piangi, o misera" (106; Weep, weep, unhappy girl). As Germont recognizes, in a *pianissimo* moment of murmured introspection, an empathetic bond now ties him to Violetta: "sento nell'anima già le tue pene" (107; In my soul I already feel your pain). The leap of a fifth to two *fortissimo* accented F's on "Coraggio, e il nobil tuo cor vincerà, ed il cor

vincerà" (107; Courage—your noble heart will overcome)
exposes Germont's futile effort to suppress this inescapable
pain; but the immediate collapse of his vocal line acknowledges the hollowness in such assurances of hope.[7] As Violetta
repeats her "Dite alla giovine" (107), his fragmented vocal line
highlights the inadequacy of the broken platitudes Germont
must fall back on in the face of her irretrievable loss, and the
moments when the two voices join briefly in thirds reempha-
size the bond of suffering that connects Germont and Violetta.

Violetta has lost the "otherness" essential to the scenario
Germont accepted in Provence, even before her plaintive "qual
figlia m'abbracciate... forte così sarò" (110; Embrace me as a
daughter... then I will be strong). To Provence, Violetta is not a
person but a social type, a demi-mondaine to be self-right-
eously execrated; but to Germont, she has become a human
being. The act of embracing Violetta, accepting her even for
an instant as his own child, crystallizes in his mind the similar
vulnerability and capacity for love that Violetta shares with his
daughter; and the terrible injustice of the sentence he must
execute is given new personal resonance. Germont the man
and Germont the instrument of society dichotomize, shaking
his sense of personal identity to its foundations.

In contrast to Duval's abrupt and silent departure in *La
Dame aux camélias*, the extended final scene in the opera powerfully illuminates the torment endured by both Germont and
Violetta. Violetta's wrenching "Morrò!.. morrò... la mia memo-
ria non fia ch'ei maledica" (I will die... I will die... do not let
him curse my memory) is almost more than Germont can bear;
and, significantly, he appropriates her melody for the first
time, as he cries, "No, generosa, vivere e lieta voi dovrete"
(112; No, generous girl, you must live and be happy). His

words are reassuring, but the barely controlled hysteria in the *allegro moderato* vocal line and pulsating string underscoring subverts these words, pointing to his subconscious understanding that such a vision of happiness is illusory.

There is an echo of Duval's "vous aurez l'estime de vous-même" (132) in Germont's urgent assurance, "Premiato il sagrifizio sarà del vostro amore, d'un'opra così nobile sarete fiera allor, sì, sì, sì" (113; Your sacrifice of love will be rewarded, you will then be proud of such a noble work, yes, yes, yes). In this new dramatic context his words reveal not contemptuous condescension but a desperate need to believe that all can still be well. However, the relentlessly falling vocal line, forced monotone repetitions, and effortful octave leap for an overly emphatic reiteration of "sì, sì, sì" all reveal the hollowness of his protestations. As Germont repeats his assurances at the conclusion of the duet, his vocal line reflects his inner struggle: he tries to break away from Violetta's melody and recapture a more self-controlled form of expression. Yet, ultimately, his line rejoins Violetta's in thirds for the final phrases of the duet in acknowledgment of an empathetic bond that can no longer be denied.

While the triumphant Duval exits without a word after Marguerite's "nous ne nous reverrons jamais sans doute, soyez heureux" (135; We will undoubtedly never see each other again, be happy), Germont and Violetta both struggle in vain to find words that can express their depth of feeling—words that might, even at this final moment, overcome the barrier society has placed between them and bring their sufferings to an end. They fall back on a hopelessly inadequate "Siate felice" (116; Be happy), but the intensity of their pain and the inarticulate helplessness that Germont and Violetta share find physical expression in a second embrace that is added to Dumas' original scene.

As Violetta sobs, "Conosca il sagrifizio" (Let him know the sacrifice), Germont's "Sì" is barely audible, and at last all efforts to find meaningful expression collapse with a mournful repetition of "felice siate" (117). When the vocal lines join in unaccompanied thirds that subtly echo the plaintive melody of "Conosca il sagrifizio," Verdi's scoring exposes the crushing futility of such a wish for happiness. The sacrifice Germont has been compelled to demand, and Violetta to make, has condemned them both, and Verdi creates an indelible image of two helpless people trapped in a world of grief and loss beyond their control.

In Dumas' play, Duval essentially disappears after his victory over Marguerite. He is seen briefly at the end of the act when Armand discovers Marguerite's flight to Paris; but Duval is not motivated by love and, pointedly, has nothing to say to his son. Germont, in contrast, has an extended *scena* in which he tries to establish a relationship with Alfredo that seems presciently modern in its transcendence of conventional bourgeois decorum. In comforting Alfredo, Germont carefully avoids the clichés of bourgeois self-righteousness. Far from expressing merely empty rhetoric, Germont's aria "Di Provenza" provides a complex psychological exploration of a man trying to find his way through the emotional chaos in which he is enmeshed.[8] Instinctively, Germont tries to turn back the clock, to return with Alfredo to an earlier time of innocence and peace: "Di Provenza il mar, il suol chi dal cor ti cancellò?" (127; Who has taken from your heart the sea and land of Provence?). The nostalgic tone of Verdi's musical setting for the aria[9] and the sense of calm in the even rhythms and elegant grace notes of the vocal line with its simple string

accompaniment portray Germont's effort to recapture something of the harmony, order, and naive simplicity of the family
life once shared with his son.

Yet, the air of sadness and loss in the relentlessly falling
phrases of Germont's vocal line suggests his unspoken recognition that a return to the past is impossible. After a confident
beginning, Germont seems at a loss for words. He can only
repeat himself, and though with added *marcate* emphasis in the
vocal line he tries to give new meaning to these repetitions, a
pianissimo denouement suggests his own sense of the inadequacy of his words (127).

As Germont tries to persuade Alfredo that in Provence
peace is still attainable, the vocal line takes on a new sense of
direction and increased emotionality in its arching phrases and
swelling dynamics: "Oh rammenta pur nel duol ch'ivi gioja a te
brillò, e che pace colà sol su te splendere ancor può" (128; Oh
remember in your grief the joy which lit you there, and that
only there can peace shine on you again). But his own inner
doubts are evidenced in the self-consciously rhetorical expan-
sion of the vocal line as he repeats his assurances. Germont is
trying to convince himself as much as Alfredo, and it is significant that he moves immediately into a climactic *con forza* cry of

"Dio mi guidò" (128; God guided me); the vocal line rises to an accented G-flat and is doubled for the first time by the orchestra. As in his earlier duet with Violetta, this appeal to the authority of God reflects Germont's own need to believe in a Providence, in a divine purpose for the suffering and grief Germont is both inflicting on others and enduring himself. The third repetition of "Dio mi guidò," this time marked *ppp* and extended with both a *rallentando* and a fermata, suggests the emptiness of his claim.

In the second verse of the aria, Germont opens his heart to his son, transcending the image of the strong bourgeois father: "Ah il tuo vecchio genitor tu non sai quanto soffrì" (129; Ah, you do not know how much your old father suffered). He is trying to relate to Alfredo on a new humanistic basis, founded not on role-playing but on mutual understanding, respect, and love. The difficulty of effecting such a change is clear, however, in Germont's inability to find a new melodic voice suited to the intimate, personal nature of his words. Germont merely repeats the initial melodic line and even returns to an echo of bourgeois decorum in his reference to "la voce dell'onor" (130; the voice of honor).

If he and Alfredo can emerge from these trials with a better personal understanding of each other, if they can build on the kind of honesty and openness of communication that Germont is trying to initiate, then perhaps they can find some hope for the future: "ma se alfin ti trovo ancor, se in me speme non fallì, Dio m'esaudì" (130; But if at last I find you again, if my hope did not fail, then God heard me). While the "Dio mi guidò" that ends the first verse of the aria reduces Germont to an instrument of divine will, there is a new emphasis in the culminating repetitions of "Dio m'esaudì" that end the second verse:

the focus is now on his prayer that God will give him the opportunity to act on his new understanding. Verdi expresses the need and hope Germont feels with an emotional adaptation of the traditional concluding *cadenza*, the vocal line exploding on a *forte* high G-flat, repeated and extended with a fermata, before a longing, *diminuendo ed allargando* descent.

Confronted with Alfredo's distracted silence, Germont becomes even more direct, asking, "Nè rispondi d'un padre all'affetto?" (131; Don't you respond to a father's affection?). Alfredo rejects his father's overture, and plaintive underscoring violins, faintly echoing Violetta's motif of love and loss, suggest Germont's recognition that his own hopes for a new future with his son have been destroyed along with her happiness. But Germont has come too far in his personal evolution to turn back, and he makes a last appeal to Alfredo, expressing his love and offering a relationship based on love and forgiveness in the *cabaletta* "No, non udrai rimproveri" (132).

While usually cut in performance and dismissed by critics as dramatically superfluous and melodically mediocre, this *cabaletta* culminates Germont's character development in the act. Pointedly subverting traditional *cabaletta* style, Germont begins not with bombast but with *pianissimo* urgency and nervous agitation as he moves through uncharted territory, trying to create a future rather than returning to the past (132; No, you will hear no reproaches; let us cover the past with oblivion: the love that guided me can forgive all).

No, non udrai rim - pro - ve - ri, copriam d'oblio il pas - sato: .... l'amor che m'ha gui -

da - to sa tutto perdo - nar.

Germont has opened his heart and offered his son a new future based on love and compassion; faced with Alfredo's complete indifference, there is no course of action left to him but increasingly frantic repetition. This pattern builds to the accelerating tempo and rising dynamics of the final *stretta*, with its fuller orchestration and six-fold "ah si t'affretta" (136; Ah, yes, hurry). But Germont's pleas are still unheeded, and, fittingly, the *cabaletta* itself ends, not with formal resolution but with Alfredo's self-absorbed interruption, "ell'è alla festa" (137; She is at the party). Germont's process of self-discovery has begun too late, and as the curtain falls the father is left alone, calling after his son, "ah ferma" (137; Ah, stop).

Although the presence of Germont at Flora's party is often ridiculed as dramatically absurd, it provides dramatic evidence of the changes he has undergone in the previous scenes. The same Germont who provoked Violetta's "Donna son io, signore" (91) with his boorish behavior now becomes her champion. Seeing how agitated Alfredo was when he departed for Paris, Germont follows out of concern for both his son and Violetta herself. He arrives at the party in time to see Alfredo publicly humiliate Violetta; and, in his outraged denunciation, Germont deliberately places himself outside the established bounds of bourgeois conduct. Despite a lingering sense of nineteenth-century paternalism in his condemnation, it is clear that Germont is acting as a human being and not as a spokesman for bourgeois values.

There is a barely maintained control in the fragmentation of Germont's heavily weighted *largo* vocal line, marked *con dignitoso fuoco* and punctuated only by *pizzicato* strings: "Di sprezzo degno sè stesso rende chi pur nell'ira la donna offende" (185; A man who offends a women, even in anger, renders himself worthy of contempt). Giving voice to his outraged disbelief, Germont's vocal line leaps an octave, underscored by the palpitating agitation of string triplets, for his *grandioso* "Dov'è mio figlio?.. più non lo vedo; in te, in te più Alfredo trovar no, no, non so." (185; Where is my son? I no longer see him; in you I can no longer find Alfredo.) The strophic regularity of his earlier vocal line, his uncertainty and search for words, his reliance on platitude and cliché are replaced by a confidence and fluid development of expression that gives Germont a new dignity, even in this moment of public humiliation and crisis. He had hoped that the new understanding gained from his suffering might bring him closer to Alfredo, that they might establish a relationship based on shared humanity rather than on social roles; but Germont sees this hope destroyed as Alfredo becomes unrecognizable in the vicious cruelty of his behavior. Germont's despair is captured in the *crescendo* of his vocal line, propelled by relentless monotone triplets that swell to high F before an agitated *accelerando* denouement (185-86).

Dov'è mio figlio?.. più non lo vedo; in te più Alfre - do tro-var, ...no, più Alfre-do trovar non so.

Although love for his daughter still prevents him from revealing the truth of Violetta's sacrifice, Germont no longer even pretends to assume the part of the aloof outsider, the bourgeois judge of the demi-mondaine's life. He shares a human bond with her, and, as he voices his own sense of helplessness at his inability to relieve her suffering or to alter the circumstances in which they are both trapped, it is significant that his vocal line blends harmoniously with those of Violetta's other friends in the ensemble that concludes the act.

By the final act, the metamorphosis of Germont is complete. Whether emancipated by his daughter's marriage or simply unable to continue to support the tortuous role he has been compelled to play, Germont at last decisively abandons social exigency and acts on the urgings of his heart. In contrast to the rigid formality of the letter Duval sends to Marguerite, Germont's letter, even given Violetta's breathless reading, evidences the fragmented urgency of a man who has come to a tumultuous decision: "Teneste la promessa... La disfida ebbe luogo... Il barone fu ferito, però migliora... Alfredo è in stranio suolo. Il vostro sagrifizio io stesso gli ho svelato. Egli a voi tornerà pel suo perdono... io pur verrò... Curatevi... mertate un avvenir migliore... Giorgio Germont." (212-13; You kept your promise... The duel took place. The Baron was wounded but is recovering... Alfredo is on foreign soil. I myself revealed your sacrifice to him. He will return to you for your pardon... I will also come... Take care of yourself... You deserve a better future... Giorgio Germont.)

Duval's ostensible remorse is no more than a hollow gesture to a dying Marguerite: "Si ma mort n'eût été certaine, ton père ne t'eût pas écrit de revenir" (180; If my death were not certain, your father would not have written you to return). Germont, however, does not know Violetta is dying; he comes himself to beg her forgiveness and to unite the lovers at last. He appears in Violetta's chamber as a man reborn. His animated entrance is underscored with energetic orchestration, and there is an eager informality in his first "Ah Violetta," a caressing effusiveness in "a stringervi qual figlia vengo al seno, o generosa" (240; to press you as a daughter to my bosom, o generous girl). He has recognized how to rectify the mistakes of the past, but his joy is frozen into horror as Germont suddenly realizes that his understanding has come too late: "Che mai dite! (Oh cielo! è ver!)" (241; What are you saying? [Heavens! it's true!]).

In contrast to the oblivious Duval, Germont cannot accept Violetta's death with detached equanimity. In a writhing expression of guilt and frustration, with the plunging phrases and explosive top E's and F's of the vocal line set against the frenzied *tutti* orchestration, Germont cries out to his son, "Di più... non lacerarmi, troppo rimorso l'alma mi divora" (241-42; Do not torture me any more, too much remorse is devouring my soul). This eruption leaves Germont in a state of enervated despair, however, murmuring on a *piano* repetition of B, "Ah mal

cauto vegliardo!.. il mal ch'io feci ora sol vedo" (242; Ah, fool-
ishly cautious old man! Only now I truly see the harm I did).

As Germont then joins in harmonic counterpoint with
Alfredo, both pray for salvation—the son's anguished "No non
morrai" (You will not die) juxtaposed with the father's "perdon-
ami lo strazio recato al tuo bel cor" (243-44; Forgive me the
torment brought to your noble heart). But Germont can no
more find peace than Alfredo can will Violetta to live. Violetta
herself has already forgiven Germont, but he cannot forgive
himself: "Finchè avrà il ciglio lagrime io piangerò" (245; As
long as my eyes have tears, I will weep). Like Rigoletto at
Gilda's death, Germont perceives a widening chasm that separates his own agony from Violetta's ascension to Heaven, and
the recognition of his irredeemable guilt gives a particular resonance to the lines "vola a beati spiriti, Iddio ti chiama" (245;
Fly to the blessed spirits, God is calling you). For Annina and
the doctor, these words are an expression of faith, but for
Germont they are also a self-condemnation, a sentence to
endure the torment of his own conscience for the remainder of
his life. He has been too late in casting off the shackles of his
society. Never again will he be able to return to the comfortable safety of social convention, but neither will he be able to
reclaim the son he sacrificed and embrace Violetta as a daughter. And the horror of this fate reverberates in his final "Oh mio
dolor" (249; Oh my sorrow).[10]

Simon Boccanegra

Simon Boccanegra (1881)[1] is a daring dramatic foray into proto-expressionism, its kaleidoscopic scenes providing an incisive exploration of the protagonist's psyche rather than a realistically developed plot. The libretto, originally adapted by Piave and later revised into its definitive form by Arrigo Boito, verges on parody—tearing to tatters the original expansive evocation of milieu in Antonio García Gutiérrez's intricately woven drama, extracting and magnifying the ludicrous series of clichés, coincidences, and incongruities that underpins the plot.

Yet, absurdities of plot mechanics become ultimately meaningless in the opera, for Verdi uses events, like the symbolic guideposts in a dream, to point the way to the unspoken world of Simon's inner self. Contemporary critics like Filippo Filippi sensed the dramatic power of the resulting psychological exploration: "There is no rhyme or reason nor any apparent justification of the strange comings and goings of the characters. . . . But what does all this matter to a composer like Verdi? Bad material does not frighten him; he knows how to clean up, beautify, and reduce it to harmonious, secure contours, and to illuminate it with his genius."[2]

Simon is a character defined in the subtext of the opera. He is not among those characters who, by conventional operatic standards, "vi fanno esclamare: 'è scolpito'" (make one exclaim, "He is finely sculpted").[3] As Verdi notes, Simon "È una parte faticosa quanto quella del Rigoletto, ma mille volte più difficile. Nel *Rigoletto* la parte è fatta, e con un po' di voce e di anima si può cavarsela bene. Nel *Boccanegra* la voce e l'anima non bastano." ([Simon] is as exhausting a part as Rigoletto, but a thousand times more difficult. In *Rigoletto* the part is already made, and with a little voice and heart one can come off well. In *Boccanegra* voice and heart are not enough.)[4] Instead, Simon is a role "a farsi" (to be made),[5] a part that must be created, rather than simply assumed, by an actor capable of plumbing the unspoken depths of the human psyche.[6] For such a characterization, traditional means of melodic expression no longer suffice, and Verdi sets off on a new musico-dramatic path.[7]

Simon exists in a spiritual abyss, his life an unending quest for redemption and peace through forgiveness and love. With the daily particulars of his life obscured by an impenetrable thicket of unanswered questions and Byronic mysteries, Simon embodies an essential and overwhelming spiritual need that transcends the details of time or place. Like an operatic

Everyman oppressed by the inescapable weight of original sin, Simon becomes a compelling image of fallen humanity desperately searching for a lost spiritual peace in a world of hatred and strife. Simon certainly embodies one of Verdi's darkest visions of human existence, and yet even here "the darkness declares the glory of light."[8] In a world of suffering and despair, Simon reaches out with Christian forgiveness, with love, with a promise of redemption that shines like a beacon to a brighter future for all humanity.

From his first appearance in the Prologue, Simon is a man swept along on a current of destiny beyond his control, trapped in a nightmare of sin and suffering, caught up in a headlong series of events that defies any realistic sense of narrative time. Paolo presses him to accept the Doge's crown, but Simon is not interested in political power.[9] He initially dismisses Paolo with a peremptory "Vaneggi?" (Are you crazy?),[10] only to relent when he is assured that as Doge he could win Fiesco's acceptance and the hand of his daughter, Maria.

Returning later, Simon again makes clear that the crown has no intrinsic value for him. Paolo has prepared the people for the new Doge's election, and Simon notes, "Suona ogni labbro il mio nome" (28; My name is on every lip). Yet, the lack of animation in this fragment of unaccompanied recitative subverts any sense of real excitement. In contrast, the next phrase leaps a full octave, filled with a new sense of urgency and hope: "O Maria! forse in breve potrai dirmi tuo sposo" (O Maria, perhaps soon you will be able to call me your husband). This hope is shattered, however, by the onslaught of Fiesco's vengeful fury over the death of his daughter: "Sul tuo capo io qui chiedea l'ira vindice del ciel" (29; On your head I was invoking the avenging fury of Heaven).

There is an almost mythic aura of primordial Sin and Punishment in the illicit love of Simon and Maria, in the surreal obscurity that envelops their past, even in Maria's mysterious death. So, too, Simon's need for forgiveness and absolution from Fiesco has become a symbolic quest for release from the miasma of original sin even before Simon makes the crushing discovery of his lover's death: "Padre mio, pietà t'imploro supplichevole a' tuoi piedi... il perdono a me concedi" (29-30; My father, supplicant at your feet I implore your mercy... grant me pardon). His vocal line is humble and self-effacing in its almost monotone phrases, yet the surging melody of the underscoring strings, woodwinds, and horn suggests the unfathomed depths of Simon's inner need.

Simon's overriding yearning for absolution strips his temporal triumphs of their inherent value. As Simon tells Fiesco of the glories he has achieved, there is a new tone of confidence in the martial phrases that carry the voice to a top F on the key word "gloria," before a *dolcissimo diminuendo* on "l'altare dell'amor." But glory, like the Doge's crown, is only offered to win Fiesco's blessing: "Sublimarmi a lei sperai sovra l'ali della gloria, strappai serti alla vittoria per l'altare dell'amor" (30-31; On wings of glory I hoped to raise myself up to her; I grasped the wreaths of victory for the altar of love). It soon becomes clear that Simon will sacrifice anything, even his hope of marriage and his very life, in order to attain absolution: "Vuoi col sangue mio placarti? qui ferisci... Sì, m'uccidi, e almen sepolta fia con me tant'ira." (33; You want my blood to placate you? Strike here! Yes, kill me, and at least let your anger be buried with me.) For Simon, Fiesco's forgiveness has become a symbol of personal redemption.

As the condition for peace, Fiesco demands the return of his granddaughter, the illegitimate child of Maria and Simon.

But Simon cannot comply, and his distress is patent as he mournfully recounts his daughter's mysterious disappearance. Like the ocean waves that carried him to the distant land where his daughter was living, the rolling phrases of his undulating, *andantino* line seem to transport Simon to another time and place, enveloping him in a hypnotic reverie as he relives that last journey: "Del mar sul lido fra gente ostile crescea nell'ombra quella gentile; crescea lontana dagli occhi miei, vegliava annosa donna su lei" (35; The child grew up in hiding on the shore of a foreign land; grew up far from my eyes, watched over by an old woman). The vocal line sinks with horror, as Simon recalls entering the empty house where his daughter should have been, only to discover her guardian dead and the child gone. Finally, with mournful resignation reflected in the drooping phrases and fading orchestration of the coda, Simon concludes, "Misera, trista, tre giorni pianse, tre giorni errò. Scomparve poscia, nè fu più vista, d'allora indarno cercata io l'ho." (36-37; Wretched and miserable, for three days she cried and wandered. After that she vanished and was seen no more, and since then I have looked in vain for her.)

Del mar sul   li - do   fra   gente o - sti - le   crescea nel - l'om-bra quel-la gen - ti - le;

There is a certain surreal tone to this sad narrative, for the vision of the miserable child and the description of events that Simon could not possibly have witnessed clearly emanate from his own imagination.[11] The reality of the child seems to disappear, replaced by a symbolic image of loss. Significantly, Simon

never even hints at the existence of a daughter until he is chal-
lenged by Fiesco, and, as soon as his narrative is concluded,
Simon abruptly changes the subject and pleads, "Coll'amor mio
saprò placarti; m'odi, ah m'odi" (38; With my love I will placate
you; ah hear me, hear me). His vocal line now rises to an emotionally sustained top F, in pointed contrast to the perfunctory
sixteenth note which climaxes "indarno cercata io l'ho" (37).
His daughter is marginalized, and it comes as no surprise,
therefore, that his ultimate reunion with her fails to provide the
redemptive love that might bring Simon peace.

For his part, Fiesco is implacable, declaring that without
the return of his granddaughter there can be no forgiveness.
He withdraws, and Simon is left to discover a loss far more
traumatic than the disappearance of his child. As Simon enters
Fiesco's deserted palace in search of Maria, his progress is
marked, with chilling dramatic irony, by the understated,
pianissimo murmuring of strings; his discovery of his lover's
corpse comes as a paralyzing shock.[12] Simon's unaccompanied
"Maria!.. Maria" (40) and Fiesco's cry of vengeful triumph are
punctuated only by the briefest crash of *allegro agitato* orchestration before the chorus' cries of "Boccanegra" are heard. Simon
has no time to give full voice to his agony of loss, for horror
and anguish, confusion and grief, are drowned in the crushing
banality of the mob's acclaim for the new Doge. Simon is
reduced to silence, and in that very silence, his life seems to
drain away.

In the course of the Prologue, Simon becomes an image of
fallen humanity, denied the peace of absolution for his sins.
His life plunges into the silence of the existential void:
twenty-five years pass between the Prologue and Act I,
twenty-five years lost in silence, twenty-five years of life ren-

dered meaningless and absurd. Then, with the first act, Verdi begins a probing psychological exploration of the man Simon has become. The plot, expressionistically episodic and compressed, becomes a metaphoric series of Rorschach tests, illuminating Simon's responses to paternal love, political power, and human forgiveness.

In Act I, Simon, as Doge, visits Amelia Grimaldi and pardons her exiled brothers.[13] His dialogue with Amelia begins with formal restraint, but a comfortable intimacy is quickly established, underscored by the courtly dance melody accompanying his "Del mondo mai le fulgide lusinghe non piangesti?" (82; Do you never shed a tear for the brilliant allurements of the world?). As their conversation proceeds apace and Amelia ingenuously confides that she is not, in fact, a Grimaldi, a flash of hope fills Simon. The reserved and aloof ruler gives way to the father, dreaming of finding his lost child. Doubled by plaintive woodwinds, his vocal line develops out of a nostalgic melodic echo of "Del mar su lido," as Simon murmurs, "Ah! se la speme, o ciel clemente, ch'or sorride all'alma mia, fosse sogno!.. estinto io sia della larva, della larva al disparir" (88; Merciful Heaven, if the hope that smiles on my soul be a dream, then let me die should it disappear). Yet, his hope remains tinged with melancholy, with the fear that this dream, too, may vanish. As Simon and Amelia join in a duet for the first time, they are still lost in their own thoughts, and the *scena* is colored by a sense of inescapable sadness.

Ah!   se   la   spe - me, o ciel cle - men - te, ch'or sor - ri - de al -l'al - ma   mi - a.

Amelia is indeed Simon's daughter, and her cry "stringi al sen... Maria che t'ama" (91-92; Clasp to your breast Maria who loves you), seems to offer the hope that through paternal love Simon can find salvation, that Maria the daughter can restore the lost innocence of Simon's love for Maria the mother.[14] But Simon's is not the same all-fulfilling love that inspires Rigoletto's "Culto, famiglia, patria, il mio universo, il mio universo è in te" (100; Religion, family, homeland, my universe, my universe is in you). The melodic simplicity of Simon's *allegro giusto*, its *dolcissimo* phrases underscored by *pizzicato* strings, undeniably evokes his happiness: "Figlia! a tal nome io palpito qual se m'aprisse i cieli" (93; Daughter, at that name I tremble as though Heaven had opened to me). Yet, at the same time, the controlled elegance in his lyrical, *bel canto* line mitigates against any real emotional transcendence.

Simon's love is tender and genuine, but it is not the stuff of spiritual redemption, and, in the final moments of the duet, the separate vocal lines maintained by Simon and Amelia reveal the divide that remains between them.[15] As Amelia departs, Simon's *dolcissimo* "Figlia" (98), the shimmering top F of the vocal line set against cascading harp arpeggios, becomes a haunting cry of yearning for the ephemeral, of yearning for paradise lost. Reality reasserts itself, however, with the jarring intrusion of Paolo's "Che rispose?" (What was her response?).[16]

Paternal love cannot fill the void of Simon's life, and it is clear in the ensuing Council scene that political power offers no greater hope.[17] The thunderous prelude that brings up the curtain, the opulence of the stage decor, the declamatory vocal scoring all insist on the heights Simon has scaled as Doge of Genoa. Significantly, however, when announcing Petrarch's plea for peace, Simon's line suddenly assumes *cantabile, dolcissimo* contours that suggest an inner need unfulfilled by the trappings of office: "ei per Venezia supplica pace" (103; He entreats peace with Venice).

Simon's call for peace is immediately submerged in Paolo's contempt, the scorn of the senators, and the sounds of rebellion from outside the palace. Genoa itself becomes a microcosm of a world defiled by incessant hatred and bloodshed. As Simon defuses the latest crises, defying the mob and ordering the senators to sheath their swords, his heightened *tessitura* captures the Doge's confident authority. With almost paternalistic condescension he notes, "Ecco le plebi" (Behold the mob), as the crowd's cries for his death turn into the acclaim of "Evviva il Doge" (115; Long live the Doge). But beneath Simon's authority is the frustration of a man crying in the wilderness. Far from embracing peace, the senators launch another round of fratricidal strife after Amelia arrives to recount the story of her abduction and miraculous escape.

At last, Simon can no longer maintain his self-control; his "Fratricidi!" (130; Fratricides!) explodes *possentemente* on a top E-flat reinforced by *fortissimo* orchestration. With new and terrible majesty, Simon offers a crushing indictment of fallen humanity, his anguished, fragmented phrases swelling almost uncontrollably to top E-flat before plunging a sixth, his visceral horror punctuated with crashing orchestration: "Plebe! Patrizi!

Popolo dalla feroce storia" (131; Plebeians! Patricians! People
of a savage history).

The feuds of the Dorias and Spinolas bear the indelible
mark of Cain, and as Simon laments a race doomed by hatred,
his line flattens into a desolate monotone. Yet, even in despair,
a vision of what might have been lingers. For Simon, the sea
now becomes a Romantic image of spiritual cleansing and
rebirth, and an infinite longing infuses his caressing phrases,
"Erede sol dell'odio dei Spinola, dei Doria, mentre v'invita esta-
tico il regno ampio dei mari" (131; Heirs only to the hatred of
the Spinolas and the Dorias, while the joyous realm of the seas
beckons). Hope is relentlessly engulfed by the recognition of
inexorable hatred, however, and the vocal line leaps to a *fortissimo* top F-flat before a headlong triplet descent doubled in
thunderous, *tutti* orchestration on "voi nei fraterni lari vi lacer-
ate il cor" (131-32; you rend your brother's heart).

Simon weeps for a world of beauty negated by human
strife, and his phrases expand in an expressive *cantabile* at a new
meno mosso tempo: "Piango su voi, sul placido raggio del vostro
clivo, là dove invan germoglia il ramo dell'ulivo. Piango sulla
mendace festa dei vostri fior." (132-33; I weep for you, for the
peaceful light on your hills, where the olive branch blossoms in
vain. I weep for the deceptive loveliness of your flowers.) His
despair is both for humanity and for himself. Simon has seen
his own life, like the city he mourns, stripped of all real mean-

ing and left a hollow shell by human hatred. At last, he seems
to bring the voice of Heaven to Earth in his transcendent
prayer for peace and Christian love: "e vo gridando: pace! e vo
gridando: amor!" (133; and I cry to you: "Peace!" And I cry to
you: "Love!").[18] During the following ensemble, Simon is con-
spicuously silent, oblivious to those around him. His attention
is turned inward now onto his own soul, onto his own need for
peace and forgiveness, and it is thus with ineffable longing that
he repeats, once only, "E vo gridando: pace! e vo gridando:
amor" (138-39).

In the final moments of the act, Simon forgives Gabriele
for his attempted assassination, leaving him his sword and asking that he remain in the palace until the plot is unmasked.
Simon's personal forgiveness cannot, however, absolve Paolo
of his crimes. Paolo has come to embody the very essence of
treachery, hatred, and destruction. His actions have precipitated the present fratricidal violence in Genoa, and for this sin
Simon consigns his former friend to the judgment of Heaven.
Simon exacts no personal vengeance, no retribution as a father
for the abduction of Amelia. Rather than using the power of his
office to unmask and punish Paolo's villainy, Simon offers an
almost cosmic indictment of evil: "Sul manigoldo impuro
piombi il tuon del mio detto: Sia maledetto!" (147; Upon the
villain let the thunder of my words fall: "Be damned!"). It is a
sentence more terrifying than any earthly power could effect,[19]

and Paolo fittingly condemns himself by repeating the curse in response to Simon's *cupo e terribile* challenge, "e tu... ripeti il giuro" (and you, repeat the oath).

In the second act, Simon's capacity for embracing the principles of love and forgiveness are further tested. The Doge enters, reading a list of those who have conspired in the latest rebellion against him, and the brooding weight of the string accompaniment makes it clear that the burden of such ceaseless conflict lies heavy on his shoulders. His first swift exchange with Amelia is full of mutual concern and tender compassion, each trying to reassure the other. But the lack of melodic scope in this virtually unaccompanied recitative makes clear that paternal love has not been able to transform Simon's existence.

This brief glimpse of their life together makes all the more striking Simon's violent reaction to Amelia's love for Gabriele. In a vocal line jagged with dismay, Simon cries, *fortissimo allegro agitato*, "Il mio nemico! Vedi: qui scritto il nome suo? Congiura co' Guelfi." (177-78; My enemy! Do you see his name written here? He is plotting with the Guelphs.) He rejects Amelia's plea for clemency with an inflexible three-fold repetition of "Nol posso" (178; I cannot). Faced with a passionate insistence by Amelia that she will share either love or death with Gabriele, Simon gives way to a surging expression of despair and loss. In an outpouring of desolation, his vocal line rises from a declamatory series of D-flats to an anguished top G-flat, followed by a dying, *pianissimo* denouement: "Una figlia ritrovo, ed un nemico a me la invola" (179-80; I regain my daughter, and an enemy steals her from me).

Simon now finds himself in Fiesco's position: his daughter is in love with a man he views as an enemy. He can freely accept Amelia's feelings for an unknown lover, but when that man is revealed to be one of his enemies, Simon must choose whether to follow Fiesco's example of hatred or his own call to peace. To accept Amelia's love for Gabriele, Simon must embrace his enemy with true forgiveness; he must yield in a way that Fiesco could not. Verdi highlights the dramatic parallels between the two men: the strings punctuating Simon's cries of loss subtly echo the passage in the Prologue when Simon offers his life to appease Fiesco (33).

It is a more difficult moment of truth than Simon ever expected. Having dismissed Amelia with the promise that a pardon might be possible if Gabriele repents, the Doge is enervated by his psychological strain. The full degree of his inner turmoil and confusion is clear in the ponderous, exhausted orchestral line underlying his own flattened, fragmented phrases: "Doge! Ancor proveran la tua clemenza i traditori?.. Di paura segno fora il castigo... M'ardono le fauci." (181-82; Doge! Will the traitors once again test your clemency? Punishment could be a sign of fear. My throat is burning.) At last, overcome by an inner struggle too great for the conscious mind to bear, Simon drinks the water that Paolo has secretly poisoned and drifts off in the release of sleep, while the orchestra provides a melancholy echo of "Figlia! a tal nome io palpito" (93).

Waking to find Gabriele again poised to assassinate him, Simon confronts his foe with fiery hatred, but he soon recognizes that this animosity is only part of an eternal cycle of human hatred and revenge: "Ah! quel padre tu ben vendicasti, che da me contristato già fu... un celeste tesor m'involasti... la mia figlia" (188-89; You have well avenged that father afflicted by me. You have stolen a heavenly treasure from me, my daughter.) When the truth about Amelia is revealed, Gabriele is stricken with remorse, and Simon determines to shatter the cycle of hate. His expansive phrases are suffused with new serenity and hope: "Sì... pace splenda ai Liguri si plachi l'odio antico" (192; (Let peace shine on Liguria and the ancient hatred be placated).[20] In a consummate musico-dramatic expression of Christian humility and self-effacement, Simon eschews the personal display of an aria, instead blending his voice in the harmonies of a trio. He extends his hand to his enemy, seeing in his own action a glimmer of hope for all humanity, a hope that out of the suffering of his own existence can come a beacon of love for those who follow: "sia d'amistanze italiche il mio sepolcro altar" (193; May my tomb be the altar of Italian brotherhood).

Concord is shattered by the sounds of the latest civil strife outside the palace. The Doge faces this struggle, as he has so many before, with calm assurance; but there is no traditional *cabaletta* as Gabriele and Simon swear to combat the rebellion. Instead, a single "All'armi!" (201-202; To arms!) serves to acknowledge that necessary violence has been accepted, though it is not embraced with joy.

By the last act, Simon has been victorious, but in place of celebration there is only sadness at the need for battle. With peace restored, Simon's captain announces to the city, "Cittadini! per ordine del Doge s'estinguano le faci e non s'offenda col clamor del trionfo i prodi estinti" (212; Citizens! At the order of the Doge, extinguish the torches and do not offend the gallant dead with the clamor of triumph).[21] At his final entrance, Simon is a man near death, debilitated by Paolo's poison, struggling to maintain coherence of thought, and engulfed by a nausea captured in the surging strings and brass of the orchestration. Breathing the cool ocean air, Simon looks out to the sea with infinite longing, the sea becoming once again an image for his own lost innocence: "Il mare!.. il mare!.. quale in rimirarlo di glorie e di sublimi rapimenti mi s'affaccian ricordi" (214-15; The sea! the sea! gazing at it brings back to my mind memories of glory and sublime joys). The wistful, undulating phrases of this reverie begin in both voice and orchestra, but Simon can no more hold onto the melodic ebb and flow than he can recover his lost past. As the orchestral current drifts on, as the vision fades, his thoughts turn to death and absolution, to the desire for cleansing and rebirth: "Ah! perchè,.. perchè in suo grembo non trovai la tomba?" (215; Why, why in its bosom did I not find my tomb?).

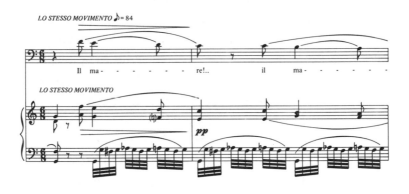

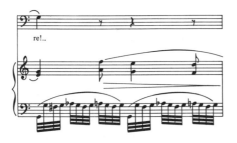

Again, hatred truncates Simon's dream, as Fiesco appears to denounce his ancient foe: "Delle faci festanti al barlume cifre arcane, funebri vedrai." (216; By the glow of festive torches, you will see mysterious, fatal signs).[22] But Fiesco's climactic cry, "Simone, i morti ti salutano" (Simon, the dead salute you), is met with the tranquil joy of Simon's "Gran Dio!.. compito è alfin di quest'alma il desio" (219; Gracious God! my soul's desire is at last fulfilled).[23] But Fiesco's declamatory D is appropriated by Simon and transformed; the clouds of fury are dissipated with a graceful descent on "desio" as the peace of *pianissimo* orchestration suffuses the line. Fiesco continues his relentless assault with the jagged phrases of "Come un fantasima" (220; Like a specter), but Simon now sees the light of salvation and cannot be drawn from his path. He placates Fiesco with the simple melody and gentle underscoring of "Di pace nunzio... Fiesco sarà" (220-21; Fiesco will be the messenger of peace).

Revealing the identity of Fiesco's lost granddaughter, Simon finds release from a lifetime of suffering. His vocal line surges to a *fortissimo*, sustained E on "In Amelia Grimaldi a me fu resa, e il nome porta della madre estinta" (222-23; As Amelia Grimaldi she was given back to me, and she bears the name of her dead mother). Simon has met hatred with love, and at last even the stony implacability of Fiesco is transformed as he recognizes the folly of his own hatred: "Piango, perchè mi parla in te del ciel... la... voce; sento rampogna atroce, sento rampogna atroce fin nella tua pietà" (224-25; I weep because the voice of Heaven speaks to me through you, and in your compassion I feel a terrible rebuke). It is now time for Simon to console the old man, and his vocal line soars in spiritual ascension as he clasps Fiesco to his heart and peace floods his soul: "Vien,..

ch'io ti... stringa al petto, o padre di Maria; balsamo all'alma mia il tuo perdon sarà." (225-26; Come, let me clasp you to my heart, father of Maria. Your forgiveness will be balm to my soul.) Their vocal lines blend with a new harmony that draws to a *ppp* conclusion, as a lifetime of animosity melts away.[24]

Simon can now end his life in peace; not only has he been released from the wheel of his suffering, but through his own actions he has brought new hope to those around him. By the time Fiesco reveals Simon's imminent death, the Doge is already transformed, his eyes fixed serenely on the glory of Heaven, his vocal line straining to escape the temporal realm: "Tutto favella, il sento, in me d'eternità" (228; I feel everything speaks to me of Eternity). This glimpse of Heaven resonates in Simon's final ethereal benediction of Amelia and Gabriele, with its imagery of redemptive martyrdom, its promise of hope for humanity through the power of Christian love: "Gran Dio, li benedici pietoso dall'empiro; a lor del mio martiro cangia le spine, le spine... in fior" (232; Merciful God, bless them from Heaven; for them change the thorns of my martyrdom into flowers). Humanity may not be able to escape the weight of primordial sin, but through individual acts of love and forgiveness the voice of God can be heard in a fallen world. The future of happiness that Simon's forgiveness has opened for Amelia and Gabriele thus offers a new hope to balance the despair Fiesco feels in recognizing the desolation of his lifetime of hatred: "Ogni letizia in terra è menzognero incanto, d'interminato pianto fonte è l'umano cor" (233-34; Every joy on Earth is a deluding spell, and the human heart is a fount of unending tears).

Leaving Genoa in the hands of Gabriele and Amelia, Simon symbolically entrusts the future of humanity to those strengthened by love, not debilitated by hate; and, as the last torches flicker out in the city, he turns to his daughter with a final *fil di voce* "Maria" (245).[25] This single name becomes both a blessing of the living and a greeting to the dead, a bridge between Earth and Heaven as Simon ascends to the Maria he lost a lifetime before, to share in the radiant love of God that he has helped to bring to the world. Turning once more to the sea, Simon is reborn, his life coming full circle as he returns to his Maria and the innocence of paradise.[26]

Otello

"Torniamo all'antico: sarà un progresso."

"Let us return to the past; it will be a step forward."[1]

Verdi's last great tragic opera, *Otello* (1887), gives new dramatic meaning to his aphorism of musical composition. With *Otello*, Verdi returns to the inspiration of Shakespeare, creating a music-drama so complex, so innovative in form and substance, that it transcends the dramatic bounds of *ottocento* opera and heralds a post-realistic approach to characterization that would not reach ascendence until the next century.[2]

The predominant movement in both opera and theatre production throughout the nineteenth century was toward the perfection of ever-greater realism on stage. Yet, operatic performance continued to include anomalous elements more suited to the metatheatrical Elizabethan tradition than to the realistic works of Augier, Ibsen, or Chekhov: the illumined auditorium, the intrusive personalities of star performers, the inevitable march to the footlights, and even the dynamics of applause and encores helped to establish an interactive connection between audience and stage.

In Shakespeare's *Othello*, metatheatricality is scripted into the text through Iago's machinations, soliloquies, and asides;[3] and when Verdi and Boito transplanted Iago to the operatic stage, he became the catalyst for a revolutionary new dramatic use of opera's metatheatrical conventions. Verdi's Jago owes no allegiance to the prevailing rules of realism; while the other characters in *Otello* function solely within the stage world of Cyprus, he blithely steps outside the drama to which he nominally belongs. Jago alone acknowledges the members of the audience, cheerfully includes them in his plans, insidiously draws them into complicity with him, and ultimately manipulates them with the same devastating skill he uses to destroy Otello. His theatrical freedom is essential, for Jago "è l'umanità, cioè una parte dell'umanità, il brutto" (is humanity, that is, a part of humanity—the ugly part).[4] He cannot be harmlessly sequestered on the stage, and it is through him that the spotlight is turned from the stage to the audience, illuminating the potential for evil in all of humanity.

Boito insists that "Jago è il vero autore del dramma, egli ne crea le fila, le raccoglie, le combina, le intreccia" (Jago is the true author of the drama; he creates the threads, gathers them, arranges them, and interweaves them).[5] From the beginning, Jago includes the spectators in his plans, leading them to view the events on stage from his perspective. Boito heightens Jago's ability to establish a special bond of intimacy and even collusion with the audience by excising Shakespeare's opening Venetian act and with it Iago's first malevolent attack on Othello. Shakespeare gives the audience full warning of Iago's villainy as the ensign awakens Desdemona's father with inflammatory cries of "Even now, now, very now, an old black ram/ Is tupping your white ewe. Arise, arise!"[6] Boito, instead, allows Jago to "look like th' innocent flower," though he is really "the serpent under't."[7]

The opera opens with the storm scene on Cyprus, where Jago reveals that his animosity toward Otello stems from what he perceives to be the injustice of the Moor's promotion of Cassio: "Quell'azzimato capitano usurpa il grado mio, il grado mio che in cento ben pugnate battaglie ho meritato" (That foppish captain usurps my rank, a rank I deserved for a hundred well-fought battles).[8] Cassio, not Otello, becomes the focus of Jago's first machinations, and the ensign's desire for revenge is superficially simple and understandable. His scheme is invitingly clever, and Jago is able to draw the audience to him by the very banality of his plot.

The original staging of this scene further facilitates Jago's intimacy with the audience. The Ricordi *Disposizione scenica* from the opera's première at La Scala indicates that Jago is able to create a bridge between stage and house through the spatial proximity afforded by the extreme forestage. While Otello, in contrast, is initially alienated from the public, delivering his famous "Esultate" from far upstage, Jago converses with Roderigo down-center and implicitly includes the audience as the silent third party in the conversation.[9]

Verdi replaces the apocalyptic violence of the storm with softly sustained strings accompanying the intimate dialogue with Roderigo, for Jago's words must be clearly heard by the

audience. His bland vocal line, devoid of emotional involvement, drains the venom from his words: "a Desdemona bella,
che nel segreto de' tuoi sogni adori, presto in uggia verranno i
foschi baci di quel selvaggio dalle gonfie labbra" (31-32; The
beautiful Desdemona, whom in your secret dreams you adore,
will soon tire of the dark kisses of that swollen-lipped savage).
Hatred becomes simple fact, for as Verdi insisted of Jago, "il fare
distratto, nonchalant, indifferente a tutto, frizzante, dicendo il
bene ed il male quasi con leggerezza ed avendo l'aria di non
pensare nemmeno a quel che dice. . . . Una figura come questa
può ingannar tutti, e fin ad un certo punto anche sua moglie."
(He appears distracted, nonchalant, indifferent to everything,
caustic, speaking good and evil lightly and having the air of not
even thinking about what he is saying. . . . A figure like this can
deceive everyone, even, up to a point, his wife.)[10]

Destruction becomes a mere game, an intellectual exercise
more in the style of comic deception than tragic annihilation,
as Jago boasts, "Se un fragil voto di femmina non è tropp'arduo
nodo pel genio mio nè... per l'inferno, giuro che quella donna
sarà tua" (32-33; If a woman's fragile vow is not too difficult a
knot for my genius, or for Hell, I swear that woman will be
yours).[11] The dancing lilt of this passage, given a playful irony
by orchestral scoring for strings, woodwinds, and horn, transforms adultery into a choreographed display of worldly sophistication. Verdi also suggests the evil concealed beneath Jago's
debonair mask, however, in the biting attack and *fortissimo*
punctuation of "nè... per l'inferno." Similarly, there is a sinister
undertone to the serpentine undulations and devilish shake in
his venomously sarcastic "ed io rimango di suo Moresca
Signoria... l'alfiere" (35; and I remain the ensign of his Moorish
Lordship).

Poco più lento

ed   io   ri - man - go di sua Mo - re - sca   Si - gno - ria ____   l'al - fie - - - re!

There is an elemental evil lurking beneath Jago's carefully crafted persona that continues to reverberate in the slithering violin figures well after Jago returns to a vocal line of urbane disinterest, and the growing clouds of smoke rising from the *fuoco di gioia* behind him symbolize his underlying malevolence (35). Emerging as if from the crashing waves of the storm, coming downstage onto the land only to disappear again into the smoke from the Cypriots' fire, Jago seems to be one with the elements, an omnipresent, primordial force. His is the power to alter the perception of reality itself, and it is fittingly ironic that the smoke which seems to embody Jago's miasmic power is celebrated by the chorus as the fire of love and faith.

This first scene is like a game of charades into which Jago lures the audience. He invites the spectators to recognize his role-playing with Roderigo and then, by moving out of earshot just as he begins to detail his plot, challenges them to guess his next move. Returning after the *fuoco di gioia*, Jago tests the audience's ability to follow the game with the cry "Roderigo, beviam! qua la tazza, capitano" (55; Roderigo, let's drink! your cup, Captain). Unlike Shakespeare's villain, Jago does not initially announce his plan: "Now, 'mongst this flock of drunkards/ Am I to put our Cassio in some action/ That may offend the isle" (II.iii.59-61). He is careful not to lose his public, however; although the role of Roderigo in the *brindisi* has surely been scripted during the *fuoco di gioia*, Jago obligingly pulls him

back to center and reiterates from this position of intimate
contact with the audience, "Ti scuoti, lo trascina a contesa; è
pronto all'ira, t'offenderà... ne seguirà tumulto" (75-76; Get
moving, draw him into a quarrel; he is quick to anger and will
offend you... an uproar will follow).[12] The tease is over, and
Jago makes sure the spectators appreciate his skill.

Jago's *brindisi* itself blends the superficial bravura of baccha-
nalian exuberance with a sinister undercurrent of relentless
pursuit. In the driving rhythms of the vocal line, in the hypnotic chromaticism and explosive violence of his exhortations,
Jago's total domination of his victim is captured: "beva, beva"
(69-70; drink, drink).[13] The delight in his song is the siren call
of destruction, and, since Jago alone abstains, there is a clear
irony in his insistence, "Fuggan dal vivido nappo i codardi...
che in cor... nascondono frodi" (71-72; Cowards who hide
deceptions in their hearts flee the bright goblet).

Inevitably, Cassio succumbs. During the melee that ensues,
Jago continues to include the audience in every step of his plot:
"Va al porto, con quanta più possa ti resta, gridando: sommossa! sommossa! Va! spargi il tumulto, l'orror." (85; Go to the
port, with all the strength you have left, crying: rebellion!
rebellion! Go! spread riot and horror.) Thus, by the time Jago is
called upon to explain the disturbance to Otello, he is able to
turn his stammering recitation of dismay into a transparent parody for the audience's amusement. Even the despairing leap of

a ninth in the vocal line becomes a burlesque of operatic exaggeration, as Jago cries, "Avessi io prima stroncati i piè che qui m'addusser" (91; Would that I had first cut off the feet that brought me here).

By the first act curtain, Jago has effected the removal of Cassio through a flawless display of mischief. The more ominous implications of his actions are carefully obscured as Jago seems to draw his plot to a close with a final "Oh! mio trionfo" (92-93; Oh! my triumph). In Shakespeare's play, the act ends with Iago urging Cassio to seek Desdemona's intervention with Othello, then confiding to the house,

> I'll pour this pestilence into his ear—
> That she repeals him for her body's lust,
> And by how much she strives to do him good,
> She shall undo her credit with the Moor.
> So will I turn her virtue into pitch,
> And out of her own goodness make the net
> That shall enmesh them all.
>
> (II.iii.356-62)

The opera, by contrast, lulls the audience into a sense of complacency by ending with the unsullied beauty of Otello and Desdemona's love duet.[14] But this peace is only a trap.

In the second act, Jago's malignity explodes with terrifying force in his blasphemous *Credo*. Verdi praised Boito's text for this monologue as "potentissimo e shaespeariano in tutto e per tutto" (most powerful and entirely Shakespearean).[15] Yet, in dramatic approach the *Credo* often seems antithetical to Shakespeare.[16] For Shakespeare's Iago, frequent soliloquies become a means to ensnare the audience; the *Credo*, by contrast, seeks not to seduce but to assault. It has none of the playful interaction of soliloquies such as Iago's "And what's he then that says I play the villain" (II.iii.336). Instead, Jago confronts the public, scorning the claims of humanism and Christianity alike, spewing forth the bile of his personal cynicism and corruption.

As he dismisses Cassio at the opening of the scene, Jago reveals his true self for the first time. In an instant, urbanity becomes malevolence as the elegant string triplets of the accompaniment are transmuted into the sinister thunder of an inexorable evil juggernaut: "Vanne; la tua meta già vedo. Ti spinge il tuo dimone e il tuo dimon son io." (113; Go! I already see your end. Your demon drives you on, and I am your demon.) He is not only Cassio's demon, however, he is the demon of all humanity. Turning to the audience, Jago steps out of the stage drama, and, as he defiantly proclaims his blasphemous inversion of faith, his belief in an "inesorato Iddio" (113-14; inexorable God), Verdi's portentous, *fortissimo* orchestration strikes the audience like a palpable blow. The challenge is given, and Jago "s'avanza verso la ribalta e si ferma in atteggiamento sardonico e fiero" (advances to the footlights and stops in a sardonic and disdainful pose).[17] With a combination of brutality and insinuation, scorn and triumph that is manifested in the juxtaposition of dynamic extremes and shifting tonalities of Verdi's scoring,[18] Jago leads the audience through a virtual catechism of evil; and at each ritual repetition of "Credo" he seems to invite different sections of the house to contradict him.

Jago not only celebrates his own fallen state, but holds himself up as an image of all humanity. Here is his first temptation of the audience, the temptation to believe that all virtue and nobility are hollow charades performed by *poseurs* as base as himself. His aggressive vocal line rises in nihilistic frenzy as Jago seeks to

demolish humanism itself: "Credo che il giusto è un istrion bef-
fardo e nel viso e nel cuor, che tutto è in lui bugiardo, lagrima,
bacio, sguardo, sacrificio ed onor" (117; I believe that the righteous man is a mocking player in face and heart, that everything
is false in him: tear, kiss, look, sacrifice, and honor).

Cre - - do che il giu-sto   è un i - stri-on   bef - far - do   e   nel vi - so e nel

cuor, che tutto è in lui bu - giar-do, la-gri-ma, ba-cio, sguardo,   sa-cri - fi - cio ed o - nor.

At last, Jago turns his attack on the very foundations of spiritual belief and religious faith. Assuming once more a mask of
studied innocence, he inquires, "Vien... dopo tanta irrision la
Morte. E poi? e poi?" (119; After so much mockery comes death.
And then? and then?). A *poco più lento* tempo with a sequence of
fading orchestral chords emphasizes the arch insinuation in
Jago's inquiry, and the long pauses offsetting "e poi?" suggest a
disingenuous look to both sides of the silent house. He gives
the audience an opportunity to respond to his question in their
own minds, only to mock their naiveté with the sardonic whisper "La Morte è il Nulla" (119; Death is Nothingness). It is his
celebration of triumphant destruction, and Jago's diabolical
delight is clear in the chilling *fortissimo allegro* explosion of "è
vecchia fola il Ciel" (119-20; Heaven is an old fable), underscored with a devilish orchestral shake and swallowed up in a
cataclysmic orchestral eruption worthy of the cannon bom-
bardment launched against Heaven by Milton's Satan.

For a character who has carefully cultivated the collusion of his audience, this gambit is dangerously alienating. Jago holds a mirror up to nature and reveals an image of nightmarish degradation, but he then transfixes the spectators by calmly setting about proving that the image is reality. Again he takes up his mask of amoral indifference, shrugging his shoulders and returning to the action of the opera, content to let the unfolding events prove his claims.[19] As he observes Cassio and Desdemona in the garden upstage, the secretive scurrying of strings in the accompaniment drains the volcanic fury from the *Credo*. The bustle of the efficient technocrat replaces the apocalyptic fury of the devil; Verdi's music captures the banality of evil.

Significantly, the dramaturgical structure of the scene draws the audience back into complicity with Jago as if the *Credo* had never happened. Cassio and Desdemona are clearly visible to the audience through the windows of the castle, and yet Jago relentlessly captions their pantomime. "Spiegando colle sue parole, quanto eseguiscono Desdemona e Cassio" (explaining with his words the actions of Desdemona and

Cassio),[20] Jago insists that the public view events through his eyes: "Già conversano insieme... ed essa inclina, sorridendo, il bel viso" (122; Already they are conversing together, and, smiling, she inclines her beautiful face). Finally, as Jago poses for greatest effect at Otello's arrival, his pointed inclusion of the audience seems almost the conspiratorial instructions of an accomplice: "Eccolo... al posto, all'opra" (123; Here he is... to my place, to work).[21]

Jago acknowledges Otello's capacity for the love, sacrifice, and honor he mocks in the Credo; and it is thus through the destruction of the noble Moor, through a merciless exposure of his frailty and potential for evil, that Jago intends to prove his vision to the audience. As the opera progresses, Jago emphasizes that his lies and insinuations merely facilitate Otello's surrender to the base side of his own nature, and Boito reinforces this sense of Otello's self-destruction by accelerating the speed of his fall. In Shakespeare's play, Othello responds to Iago's warning against the "green-ey'd monster" of jealousy with the cry, "Away at once with love or jealousy" (III.iii.166,192); but in the opera, Otello's response already has an ominous fatality about it: "amore e gelosia vadan dispersi insieme" (132; together love and jealousy be dissolved).

As Jago first begins to raise suspicion of Cassio in Otello's mind, his play-acting takes on new transparency for the audience. The Credo has enhanced the audience's understanding of Jago and has added a new sensitivity to the nuances of his masquerade. The studied calm of Jago's music as he murmurs "Ciò m'accora" (124; That worries me), the exaggerated nonchalance of his inquiry "Cassio, nei primi dì del vostro amor, Desdemona non conosceva?" (125; Didn't Cassio, in the first days of your love, know Desdemona?), the infuriating reticence in his seemingly uncomprehending reiteration of Otello's questions, all signal a carefully calculated role.

The unshakable serenity of his vocal line is betrayed by Jago's aggressive pursuit of Otello in the staging.[22] Like a game of cat-and-mouse, Jago follows his quarry, finally cornering Otello far downstage as if to include the public in the irony of "Temete, signor, la gelosia" (130; Beware jealousy, my lord). Here, too, Verdi's scoring offers a subtle metatheatrical joke, for there is an echo of Jago's first act "ed io rimango" (35) in the hypnotic, serpentine undulation and culminating shake of "È un'idra fosca, livida, cieca, col suo veleno sè stessa attosca, vivida piaga le squarcia il seno" (131; It is a dark hydra, livid, blind, that with its own venom poisons itself and rends its own breast with gaping wounds).

In this context, Jago's "vigilate" (134; watch carefully) has a double meaning—just as Otello is urged to watch Desdemona, so the audience is urged to watch Otello. Otello must choose between two visions of his wife: the reality he can see in the garden and hear in the innocence of the lyrical choral ode; and the illusion that lurks only in his mind and insinuates itself, like Jago's insidious vocal line, into the beauty of the scene. As Jago triumphantly announces to the audience, "Beltà ed amor... in dolce inno concordi!.. I vostri infrangerò soavi accordi." (150-52; Beauty and love in the concord of sweet song! Your gentle chords I will shatter.) Ensnared by Jago's deft duplicity, Otello can no longer differentiate illusion from reality. Though he declares, "S'ella m'inganna, il ciel sè stesso irride" (151-52; If she is deceiving me, Heaven mocks itself), Desdemona's entrance leads inevitably to his renunciation of love during the ensuing quartet: "ella è perduta e irriso io sono" (165; She is lost, and I am mocked).

The quartet also provides the audience with another glimpse of the true Jago, as he brutally forces Emilia to relinquish Desdemona's handkerchief. His vocal line during this exchange is devoid of melodic contour, the biting fragmentation of his *staccato* line depicting the spiritual wasteland that is Jago's soul. The scene offers a brief but telling moment of dramatic characterization, and the staging of the quartet emphasizes its importance, ensuring that the dialogue between Jago and Emilia at stage-right commands equal attention with the lamentations of Otello and Desdemona at stage-left: "il dialogo fra Emilia e Jago deve essere detto in tono sommesso, ma in pari tempo deve spiccare chiaramente" (the dialogue between Emilia and Jago should be spoken in a low tone, but at the same time must stand out clearly).[23] For a moment, Jago seems to lose control over the audience's perception of the drama, but he quickly reasserts himself, stepping forward with confident intimacy to declare, "Già la mia brama conquido, ed ora su questa trama Jago lavora" (165-66; Already I gain what I desire, and Jago is now working on this plot). He is performing for his public again, and thus his vocal line takes on new suavity and melodic scope, providing a filigreed counterpoint to the suffering of Otello and Desdemona.

This metatheatrical connection with the audience continues even after Otello and Jago are left alone on the stage, for while Otello collapses in a chair, Jago shares with the house the next step in his plan: "Con questi fili tramerò la prova del peccato d'amor. Nella dimora di Cassio ciò s'asconda... Il mio velen lavora." (170; With these threads I will weave the proof of the sin of love. In Cassio's residence it shall be hidden... My poison is working.) Jago is successful in loosing the maelstrom of Otello's submerged violence, ironically being caught in the storm of his own making when Otello attacks him.

For his plan to succeed, Jago must now refocus Otello's volcanic potential. With consummate skill, he first gains control of the scene, draining Otello's rage, and reducing the Moor to near paralysis. Jago offers no proof of Desdemona's infidelity; indeed, a sardonic unison shake by bassoon and cello emphasizes not only his demonic torture of his victim but also his devilish joke, as Jago demands, "E qual certezza v'abbisogna? Avvinti verderli forse?.. Ardua impresa sarebbe." (183-84; And what certainty do you require? To see them embracing, perhaps? That would be a difficult enterprise.) It certainly would be difficult to find Desdemona and Cassio embracing, as Jago well knows.

Instead of proof, then, Jago relates Cassio's ostensible dream of love. Through the nocturnal sensuality, the sinuous mystery of his *mezza voce* vocal line, doubled with *pianissimo* strings, Jago seems to transform the very reality of the stage, conjuring a fantastic dream realm into which Otello sleepwalks: "Era la notte, Cassio dormia, gli stavo accanto" (186; It was nighttime, Cassio slept, and I was close beside him). The scoring for this scene goes beyond the evocation of mood and setting to suggest the hypnotic power Jago exerts over his victim.

The snake becomes the charmer as Jago draws Otello into an ever-deeper trance, pouring into his mind Cassio's suggestive,

disembodied voice in a white monotone that builds to a quiver-
ing climax of orgasmic chromaticism "Desdemona soave! Il nos-
tro amor s'asconda. Cauti vegliamo! l'estasi del ciel tutto
m'innonda." (187; Sweet Desdemona! Our love be hidden. Let
us watch carefully! Heavenly ecstasy overwhelms me.)

Jago refuses to release Otello from his spell even at the end
of this dream scene, and a continued sense of paralysis is discernable in the Moor's monotone "Oh! mostruosa colpa"
(188-89; Oh! monstrous guilt). Finally, with a virtual mocking
smirk to the audience, Jago delivers his final blow: "Quel faz-
zoletto ieri (certo ne son) lo vidi in man di Cassio" (190-91;
That handkerchief I saw yesterday [I am certain] in Cassio's
hand). As by a clap of the hands, Otello is instantly freed from
his trance, and Jago stands aside while the Moor proves the
potential baseness of humanity in his hatred and rage. Jago has
loosed the hydra within Otello, and this serpent of evil is
embodied in the writhing triplets of the clarinets, bassoons,
and horns underscoring Otello's declamatory "Sì, pel ciel" (193;
Yes, by Heaven). Fittingly, however, Jago first introduces the
hydra melody into the vocal line; as he gives voice to the
triplet rhythms of the orchestra, he and the hydra become one.

Jago embodies the evil in all humanity, and his power
seems to overwhelm Otello. He prevents the Moor from rising
after the first verse of "Sì, pel ciel," kneeling beside him, lead-

ing his thoughts to bloody deeds.[24] Through the ceremonial image of these two men together on their knees downstage, the audience is drawn into a blasphemous, unholy union, a union presided over by Jago's cruel "Dio vendicator" (201; God the Avenger), a union that embodies the Satanic inversion of honor, loyalty, and love proclaimed in the *Credo*. By the end of the duet, Otello's metamorphosis is complete. With the oath of revenge, "per la Morte" (198; by Death), Otello's vocal line joins in the hydra's triplet melody, and Jago is content to pass the melodic initiative to the Moor. At last, in a moment of supreme musical irony, Otello triumphantly rises to a *fortissimo* high A while Jago offers deferential harmonic support. Otello has irrevocably embraced the evil within himself; the victory belongs to Jago.

Otello has fallen, but Jago's plot is far from over: just as Cassio was only a means to the greater temptation of Otello, so Otello himself is a means to Jago's ultimate temptation of the spectators. Jago tempts them to accept his evil vision of humanity, to acknowledge him as an image of themselves. Throughout the opera, Jago entices the audience to join him in his game, to participate in his plot, to view the events on stage as an intellectual exercise rather than a human tragedy. This temptation can succeed only if he can block any emotional involvement with the characters on stage. The humiliation of Desdemona when Otello denounces her as "quella vil cortigiana che è la sposa d'Otello" (224-25; that base strumpet who is the wife of Otello) threatens to release the spectators' compassion, and Jago must thus use the following eavesdropping scene to pull the audience back to his own cerebral perspective.

The very nature of an eavesdropping scene invites the audience to assume a position of intellectual superiority, for it perceives a totality of which the characters on stage hear only a part. Jago panders to this sense of superiority, providing the spectators with a stream of clues and subtle double entendres that feeds their sense of intellectual mastery over the intricacies of the game. The signature shakes that punctuate his otherwise courtly greeting of Cassio and recur in the playful *allegro moderato* with which he leads Cassio to boast of his amorous adventures with Bianca (236) thus serve as a signal to the audience of Jago's familiar deception. Similarly, the syncopated rhythms of the descending string accompaniment during Jago's "Essa t'avvince coi vaghi rai" (236; She enthralls you with her enchanting looks) slyly remind the audience of both Cassio's tenuous position and the treacherous quicksand that constitutes Otello's reality. It is so important for Jago to bind the audience to him that he even indulges in a pointedly ironic warning about the significance of Desdemona's handkerchief, a warning which seems to insist to the public that he is observing the rules of fair play: "bada ai deliri vani e bugiardi. Questa è una ragna." (245; Beware of empty and deceiving raptures. This is a cobweb.) His admonition applies equally to Cassio and Otello, and the playful *staccato* gallop of the *allegro brillante* scoring conveys Jago's mocking certainty that both men will remain deaf to the significance of his words.

While the oblivious Cassio tries to carry on a realistic dialogue, Jago metatheatrically leaps in and out of the scene, providing a running commentary in his asides to the audience, captioning Otello's perfectly visible action in his own words: "Otello origlia. Ei s'avvicina con mosse accorte." (243; Otello is eavesdropping. He draws near with wary movements.) Jago insists on the artifice of the scene, reminding the audience it is viewing a theatrical performance. With each aside, he momentarily shatters the realistic illusion of the stage action and, in doing so, distances the audience from emotional involvement in the drama. His garrulousness is thus merely manipulation, and in the moments when his dialogue with Cassio becomes inaudible to the audience as well as to Otello, Jago pointedly reminds his public that it hears and understands only what he chooses to share. At his discretion, the audience is left as confused as Otello: "Le parole non odo... Lasso! e udir le vorrei! Dove son giunto." (241; I cannot hear the words. Alas! I would like to hear them! What has become of me.)

As the third act builds to its conclusion, Jago maintains complete control. He insidiously suggests bringing Desdemona before the Venetian ambassadors, as if he is certain that Otello will lose control and humiliate himself. He undermines Otello with Lodovico, responding to the ambassador's question "Quest'è dunque l'eroe?" (This is the hero?) with an ironic, "È quel ch'egli è" (266; He is what he is). Even when Otello's recall to Venice threatens to derail his scheme, Jago simply acts with increased dynamism, pushing Otello to murder Desdemona and instructing Roderigo to dispatch Cassio. As Boito writes, "Così, Jago dopo essere stato, per un istante solo, sopraffatto da un avvenimento che non era in suo potere, (la lettera che richiama Otello a Venezia) riannoda subito, con una rapidità ed una energia senza pari, tutti i fili della tragedia e torna a far sua la catastrofe, ed anzi si vale dell'avvenimento imprevvisto per accelerare vertiginosamente il corso del disastro finale." (Thus Jago, having been overcome for only a moment by an event that was not within his control [the letter that recalls Otello to Venice], suddenly regathers the threads of the tragedy with unparalleled speed and energy, pursuing his catastrophe, and even profiting from the unforseen event to accelerate at breakneck speed the course of the final disaster.)[25]

The finale of the act was a source of considerable concern for Verdi,[26] and it certainly appears to be an anomalous interval of dramatic stasis if considered from a realistic perspective. Considered as part of Jago's metatheatrical manipulation of the audience, however, the finale is a master stroke. Only by reducing the other characters to an inanimate tableau, only by minimizing the limpid expression of suffering in Desdemona's vocal line, only by turning the entire stage into a backdrop for his own actions, can Jago command the audience's full attention and maintain his intellectual control during this moment of emotional effusion. As Verdi himself insists, "non vi può essere verità scenica, né effetto, se non si arriva ad isolare completamente Jago; a far sì che gli occhi del pubblico siano rivolti a lui solo, che le sue parole, non la voce, dominino su tutto e si senta sotto un mormorio indistinto ed anche inesatto se volete! Inesatto! Questa parola farebbe rizzare i capelli in testa ad un musicista, ma non importa." (There can be neither truth nor effect on stage unless one can completely isolate Jago; make the eyes of the public fasten on him alone, make his words, not his voice, dominate everything so that one hears beneath only an indistinct and inexact murmur, if you will. Inexact! That word would make the hair on a musician's head stand on end, but no matter.)[27]

Within the frozen tableau of the ensemble, Jago is the only active force, controlling the other characters like a puppeteer, demanding the audience's attention through both his words and the theatricality of his movement as he crosses first to Otello and then to Roderigo.[28] The master manipulator is at work, both on stage and in the house, surreptitiously alienating the audience from Desdemona and her suffering. Finally, as he ostensibly mocks Roderigo's gullibility, Jago is able to turn directly to the house, implicitly scorning the spectators' self-deluding mirage of human nobility: "corri al miraggio! il fragile tuo senno ha già confuso un sogno menzogner." (306-309; Run to your mirage! Your fragile sense has already confused a false dream.) It is a cutting indictment, but one unfortunately given little musical prominence or individuality.

By the end of the act, however, Jago exults with savage triumph in the vindication of his belief in the inherent evil of humanity. As the hollow cries of "Viva Otello" echo offstage, Jago declaims on a biting series of D-flats, "L'eco della vittoria porge sua laude estrema" (321; The echo of victory delivers its final hymn of praise). The lion has been vanquished, and as Jago approaches the prostrate Otello he challenges the audience with a vitriolic vocal line doubled by a hammering orchestration: "Chi può vietar che questa fronte prema col mio tallone?" (322; Who can prevent me from crushing this brow with my heel?). Pressing his foot down on the Moor, Jago symbolically crushes all opposition to his evil *Credo*, revelling in his destructive power with a diabolical shake on "Ecco il Leone" (322; Here is the lion).[29]

Ec - co il Le - o - ne!..

Significantly, however, only after Jago withdraws from the stage action do the members of the audience feel the full effects of his schemes; only in the fourth act do they viscerally experience the true horror of the events in which they have participated. At the deaths of Desdemona and Otello there is no ironic commentator, no metatheatrical agent eager to help the audience maintain an emotional alienation. The game suddenly becomes the almost unbearable reality of human suffering and loss. Feeling replaces cerebration, and it is ultimately through their tears that the spectators are freed from Jago's spell, freed from the tyranny of his intellectual cynicism. Only now can they look deep within themselves and wonder how they could have become so enmeshed in Jago's net, how they could have so blinded themselves to the terrible human cost of Jago's game.

At the end of *Otello*, the audience is denied the comfort that Shakespeare provides with the arrest and impending punishment of Iago. Jago escapes in the final moments of the opera, and the audience is forced to recognize that the dark side of human nature he embodies is not so easily neutralized. The tempter will always exist, luring humanity to self-destruction. But for every impulse to evil there is also an impulse to good; for every Jago, there is a Desdemona. As G. Wilson Knight notes of Shakespeare's play, "the beauties of the *Othello* world are not finally disintegrated: they make 'a swan-like end, fading in music.'"[30] And so the opera ends not with cynicism and hatred, but with a haunting echo of the first act duet between Otello and Desdemona, with a musical affirmation of humanity's capacity for nobility and love, with a transcendent harmony that Jago could never hear.

Appendix: Plot Synopses

Nabucco

ACT I: JERUSALEM

Inside the temple of Solomon, the Hebrews bewail the fall of Jerusalem to Nabucco's advancing troops and pray for divine intervention. The High Priest Zaccaria declares that God is with them and has delivered Nabucco's daughter Fenena into their hands as a hostage. Ismaele, nephew of the King of Jerusalem, announces that the Assyrian armies are at hand. Zaccaria places Fenena in Ismaele's custody, and the Hebrews rush off to battle.

Unknown to Zaccaria, Fenena and Ismaele are in love. When Ismaele had been the Hebrew ambassador in Babylon, Fenena had rescued him from prison, and now he hopes to save her. The lovers are interrupted by Abigaille, a slave thought to be Nabucco's older daughter, who arrives at the temple with a band of disguised Assyrian soldiers. Abigaille, too, has been in love with Ismaele and offers to save the Hebrews if he will now return her love. Ismaele refuses, and Abigaille vows vengeance as the panic-stricken Hebrews flood back into the temple.

Nabucco rides his horse onto the very steps of the temple, but Zaccaria threatens to kill Fenena if the king defiles the sanctuary. Nabucco dismounts, warning of the terrible fury of his revenge and commands the Hebrews to yield. Zaccaria raises his dagger to kill Fenena, but Ismaele seizes the weapon and frees her. As Zaccaria calls down the wrath of God for Ismaele's treachery, Abigaille vows revenge for her spurned love, Ismaele and Fenena lament their fate, and Nabucco exultantly orders the sacking of the temple.

ACT II: THE GODLESS MAN

Scene 1: Nabucco's Royal Palace in Babylon

Nabucco continues his conquests, having appointed Fenena regent of Assyria. Abigaille, furious at this insult, now discovers that she is not really the king's daughter, but a slave. She looses her fury against Nabucco, Fenena, and all of Assyria, only then to think mournfully of a time when she, too, felt love and compassion. The High Priest of Baal reports that Fenena is freeing the Hebrew captives, and Abigaille triumphantly accepts his proposal to seize the crown.

Scene 2: A Hallway in Nabucco's Palace

Zaccaria, captured along with the Hebrews, prays to God as he prepares to preside over Fenena's conversion to Judaism. The Hebrews excoriate Ismaele for his betrayal, but Zaccaria reveals that since Fenena has converted, Ismaele has actually saved a Hebrew life. The High Priest of Baal and his men arrive declaring that Nabucco is dead and that Abigaille will be queen.

As Abigaille snatches the crown from Fenena, Nabucco himself appears and places the crown on his own head. Infuriated by the treachery of Abigaille and the priests, the defiance of Zaccaria, and the revelation that Fenena is a Hebrew, Nabucco cries that all will worship him, that he is no longer king, but God. He is struck by a bolt of lightning from Heaven and drifts into delirium, while Zaccaria declares that the godless man has been punished. Abigaille seizes the crown, vowing to preserve the glory of Assyria.

ACT III: THE PROPHECY

Scene 1: The Hanging Gardens of Babylon

Abigaille has ascended the throne, and the priests of Baal demand the execution of the Hebrews. Nabucco enters, his mind wandering. Abigaille taunts him for his cowardice and lack of will and quickly coerces him into signing the Hebrews' death warrant. Realizing too late that his decree dooms Fenena as well, Nabucco tries to stop Abigaille, denouncing her as a slave. But Abigaille destroys the incriminating document, and Nabucco can only plead for mercy. Abigaille is implacable and has Nabucco taken prisoner.

Scene 2: The Bank of the River Euphrates

The captive Hebrews long for their lost homeland, and Zaccaria prophesies the fall of Babylon.

ACT IV: THE SHATTERED IDOL

Scene 1: An Apartment in Nabucco's Palace

Nabucco awakens from a nightmare and calls for an attack on Zion, but seeing Fenena being led away to execution out-

side his window, he realizes that he is a prisoner. Falling to his
knees, he prays to God for forgiveness, and his sanity is
restored. His loyal troops enter and together they rush off to
save Fenena.

Scene 2: The Hanging Gardens of Babylon

As she is taken to her martyrdom, Fenena prays serenely to
God. Nabucco and his troops burst on the scene, and the king
orders the idol of Baal destroyed. Before the soldiers can touch
it, however, the statue is toppled and shattered by the power of
God. Nabucco frees the Hebrews, vowing to rebuild the temple of Solomon and leading a prayer in praise of the one, true
God. Abigaille, who has taken poison, enters and prays for
divine mercy. As she dies, Zaccaria announces that in serving
God, Nabucco will be the king of kings.

Ernani

ACT I: THE BANDIT

Scene 1: The Bandit Camp in the Mountains of Aragon

A Spanish noble by birth, Don Juan of Aragon has been driven by a family feud with the king to become a renegade bandit chief under the alias Ernani. As his men celebrate their carefree life, Ernani reveals his love for Elvira, lamenting her impending marriage to her aged guardian, Don Ruy Gomez de Silva. His men vow to help him save Elvira, and they depart for Silva's castle.

Scene 2: Elvira's Apartment in the Castle

Elvira dreams of being rescued by Ernani. Carlo, king of Spain, arrives incognito and declares his love, but Elvira spurns his advances. Carlo threatens to abduct her, but Ernani bursts into the room through a secret panel. He defiantly confronts Carlo, who contemptuously advises the bandit to flee for his life. Silva now arrives to discover Elvira with both men in her apartment. He summons his followers and demands a duel until it is revealed that one of the seducers is the king. Silva begs pardon from his sovereign, and Carlo shields Ernani from the old man's wrath by announcing that the bandit is a member of his royal retinue. Declaring that he has come to discuss with Silva the impending election of a new Holy Roman Emperor, Carlo bids Ernani depart, while the bandit declares that his hatred for his foe remains undiminished.

Act II: THE HOST

In the great hall of Silva's castle, Elvira and her attendants prepare for the wedding. Elvira believes Ernani has been killed by the king's forces. Ernani himself appears, disguised as a monk, and Silva extends his hospitality to the traveler. When Elvira enters in her bridal dress, Ernani throws off his disguise and offers his life as a wedding present to his faithless lover. Silva insists that as his guest Ernani will not be turned over to the king. He goes to check the castle defenses, and Elvira confesses that she had intended to kill herself at the altar. Ernani is striken with remorse for his jealousy, and the two embrace as Silva returns. Silva vows vengeance on his treacherous guest, but at that moment Carlo and his men arrive at the castle.

Honoring his obligations as a host, Silva protects Ernani from the king by hiding the bandit in a secret compartment behind a portrait. He greets Carlo with deference, but refuses to yield up his guest. Enraged, Carlo threatens to destroy the castle. Elvira pleads for mercy, and the king decides to take her with him as an ostensible hostage. Silva refuses to betray his code of honor, and Carlo departs with Elvira, promising her a future of happiness and love.

Learning that Carlo has carried off Elvira, Ernani reveals to Silva that the king is their rival. He pleads with Silva to spare his life long enough for him to be avenged on Carlo. Handing Silva a hunting horn, Ernani swears to forfeit his life to Silva whenever the old man sounds it.

ACT III: THE PARDON

Outside the tomb of Charlemagne at Aix-la-Chapelle, Carlo awaits the electors' choice of a new Holy Roman

Emperor. He recognizes that his youthful dreams were only delusions and embraces the clemency and virtue of royal majesty that will make his name immortal.

Carlo conceals himself in the tomb as Ernani, Silva, and the conspirators enter. They draw lots to select the man who will assassinate the king, and Ernani wins. Silva offers the bandit's life in exchange for the honor, but Ernani refuses. Three cannon shots signal that Carlo has been elected emperor, and he emerges from the tomb to confront his foes while Elvira and a crowd of electors, courtiers, and soldiers flood the scene.

The emperor orders all noble conspirators executed and the others imprisoned. Ernani declares his right to death, revealing that he is Don Juan of Aragon, and Elvira begs Carlo for mercy. Inspired by the spirit of Charlemagne, Carlo renounces his plans for vengeance. He pardons the conspirators and blesses the marriage of Ernani and Elvira. Everyone hails the new emperor, except for Silva, who remains intent on revenge.

ACT IV: THE MASK

Don Juan's palace in Aragon is ablaze with the festivities of a ball celebrating the marriage of Elvira and the former bandit. The lovers stroll onto the terrace, declaring the joy they have found with each other. A horn is heard in the distance, and Ernani, horrified, realizes that Silva is exacting his revenge. Feigning illness, Ernani sends Elvira for some medicine. A masked figure appears; it is Silva, demanding that Ernani keep his pledge. He is deaf to all pleas, and at last Ernani stabs himself. Elvira collapses on her lover's corpse, while Silva voices his vindictive triumph.

Macbeth

Scene 1: A Wood, amidst Thunder and Lightning

Three groups of witches meet on a stormy heath, revelling in their malicious spells. A drum heralds the arrival of Macbeth and Banco, generals in the army of the Scottish king, Duncano. The witches hail Macbeth as Thane of Glamis, Thane of Cawdor, and King of Scotland. Before vanishing, they also prophesy that Macduff will be father to a line of kings. Messengers immediately arrive from Duncano to announce that the king has elevated Macbeth to be Thane of Cawdor. With two of the prophecies fulfilled, Macbeth is terrified by the thought of Duncano's murder and determines to let fate take its course without action on his part. As the men leave, the witches return to plan their next meeting with Macbeth.

Scene 2: A Hall in Macbeth's Castle

Lady Macbeth reads a letter from her husband detailing the witches' prophecies and resolves to give Macbeth the courage to kill Duncano and seize the throne. A messenger arrives with news that the king will spend the night at the castle, and Lady Macbeth invokes the spirits of darkness to aid her murderous intentions. Macbeth arrives, and the two agree on the assassination.

The king and his entourage are taken to their chambers. Alone, Macbeth imagines a dagger stained with his sovereign's blood. Suppressing his horror, he enters the king's apartment.

He returns to meet Lady Macbeth after the murder, terrified by his deed and the certainty of his own damnation. Unable to persuade him to return to Duncano's room, Lady Macbeth seizes the dagger herself and hastens off to besmear the guards with blood. A knocking is heard, and Lady Macbeth drags her husband away to wash Duncano's blood from their hands.

Banco and Macduff enter and, discovering the king's murder, awaken the castle. Macbeth, Lady Macbeth, and the assembled company call down the curse of Heaven on the unknown assassin.

ACT II

Scene 1: A Room in Macbeth's Castle

Macbeth is now king, but he cannot forget the witches' prophecy that Banco will be father to a succeeding line of kings. Macbeth shares with his wife his plan to secure his own future by murdering Banco and his son, Fleance. Macbeth departs, and Lady Macbeth, alone, reflects on the necessity of another crime and rejoices at the prospect of a secure throne.

Scene 2: A Park with Macbeth's Castle in the Distance

The murderers hired by Macbeth ambush and kill Banco, but Fleance escapes.

Scene 3: The Banquet Hall in Macbeth's Castle

Macbeth greets his noble guests, and Lady Macbeth sings a drinking song. One of the murderers surreptitiously reports

Banco's death and Fleance's escape to Macbeth. Macbeth returns to the company, offering a toast to the absent Banco but then sees the ghost of Banco occupying his own royal chair. Macbeth is terrified; his guests, who cannot see the ghost, are confounded by their king's unaccountable ravings. Lady Macbeth tries to restore the joviality of the evening with another verse of her drinking song, but the ghost reappears, bringing on an even more violent outburst from Macbeth. The guests express their dark suspicions and Macduff determines to flee the country, while Macbeth declares that he will compel the witches to reveal the future to him.

ACT III

In their secret cave, the witches dance around a boiling cauldron. When Macbeth arrives and demands that they answer his questions, the witches conjure a series of apparitions. First, a helmeted head rises from the cauldron, warning, "Beware Macduff." Next, a bloody child appears with the assurance, "None born of woman shall harm you." Third, a crowned child with a tree in his hand emerges, declaring, "You shall be glorious and invincible until you see Birnam Wood come against you." At last, Macbeth asks whether Banco's heirs will ascend the throne, and the witches respond with a series of eight apparitional kings followed by Banco, who holds a mirror revealing an endless procession of royal progeny. Overcome, Macbeth sinks unconscious to the ground, and the witches dance around him.

The witches disappear, and Macbeth recovers as his wife enters. Macbeth tells her what he has seen, and she urges him to take swift and bloody action. Together, they vow to put Macduff's castle to the sword and wreak a terrible vengeance on their foes.

ACT IV

Scene 1: A Deserted Spot on the Scottish Border

Macduff mourns the slaughter of his family, and the Scottish exiles lament their country's oppression under the tyranny of the usurper Macbeth. Duncano's son Malcolm arrives leading an English army, and the exiles, carrying branches from Birnam Wood as camouflage, march with him against Macbeth.

Scene 2: A Hall in Macbeth's Castle

Lady Macbeth's doctor and a gentlewoman watch as their mistress appears, sleepwalking. Unable to bear the weight of her guilty secret, Lady Macbeth experiences a nightmarish reenactment of Duncano's murder as she tries in vain to clean off the blood she imagines on her hands.

Scene 3: Another Room in Macbeth's Castle

Macbeth faces his impending battle with Malcolm and the English army defiantly. Although he is confident of victory, he recognizes that his actions have desiccated his life, draining it of love, compassion, and respect. When the gentlewoman brings word of Lady Macbeth's death, he greets the news with nihilistic abandon. As his soldiers announce the advance of Birnam Wood, Macbeth rushes out to find death or glory.

Scene 4: A Plain

In the midst of the battle, Macbeth enters, pursued by Macduff. Macbeth warns his opponent to flee, declaring that none born of woman may harm him; but Macduff reveals that his was untimely ripped from his mother's womb. Macbeth realizes that he is doomed, and the two men exit in fierce combat. Malcolm and his men enter, declaring their victory and announcing that Macduff has killed Macbeth. Peace and order are restored, and Malcolm, the new king, promises a joyful future for Scotland.

Rigoletto

Scene 1: The Duke of Mantua's Palace

A ball is in progress, and the libertine Duke proclaims that in his pursuit of pleasure one woman is as good as another. He has seen a charming young girl at church and plans to seduce her, but for the moment he makes love to the Countess Ceprano. The Duke's hunchbacked jester, Rigoletto, mocks the countess' hapless husband, provoking the rage of the courtiers.

Monterone, father of one of the Duke's earlier conquests, enters to denounce the man who dishonored his child. Rigoletto jeers at him, and Monterone calls down a father's curse on the jester, paralyzing him with horror.

Scene 2: An Alley with Rigoletto's Walled Garden on One Side and the Ceprano Palace on the Other

Haunted by Monterone's curse, Rigoletto returns to his home that night. In the street he meets the assassin Sparafucile, who offers his services, but Rigoletto dismisses him. Rigoletto rages against the dehumanizing contempt with which the court treats him, but he is filled with joy as he enters the garden and greets his daughter, Gilda. Tearfully, he tells Gilda about her late mother, declaring that his daughter is now his entire world. He warns her never to leave the house except to go to church and orders her nurse to guard her carefully. Hearing noises in the street, Rigoletto goes to investigate, and the Duke slips into the garden. Rigoletto then departs after a final farewell and warning to the nurse.

The Duke, disguised as a student, passionately declares his love to Gilda, the young woman he saw in church. She returns his feelings, and they swear their eternal devotion. The courtiers enter in the street, and the Duke departs, leaving Gilda to dream of her dear beloved as she goes inside.

The courtiers plot their revenge on Rigoletto, planning to kidnap Gilda, whom they believe to be his mistress. Rigoletto returns, but they convince him that they intend to abduct the Countess Ceprano. Relieved, Rigoletto agrees to help. He is blindfolded and holds the ladder as the courtiers scale the wall of his own garden and carry off his daughter. Realizing he has been deceived, Rigoletto rushes into his house, searching frantically for Gilda. finding her gone, he cries, "The curse," as he falls unconscious.

ACT II

The Duke has returned to his palace, distraught over Gilda's disappearance. The courtiers announce that they have kidnapped Rigoletto's "mistress" and brought her to the Duke's chambers. Realizing that the girl is Gilda, he hastens to her.

Struggling to affect nonchalant indifference, Rigoletto enters in search of his daughter. The courtiers tell him that the Duke is asleep, but Rigoletto quickly realizes that he is with Gilda. In desperation, Rigoletto cries that he wants his daughter returned, throwing himself toward the door to the Duke's chambers. Overpowered by the courtiers, he first curses them, then begs pity, but in vain.

When Gilda enters, Rigoletto thinks for a moment that his prayers have been answered, but soon discovers that she has become the Duke's latest conquest. Rigoletto orders the courtiers from the room and tries to comfort his daughter as she relates the story of her love for the young student she saw at church and her subsequent abduction.

Monterone is led to his execution, and Rigoletto vows to avenge them both. Gilda still loves the Duke and pleads with her father to spare his life, but Rigoletto is implacable.

ACT III

Rigoletto brings his daughter to the half-ruined inn on the deserted bank of the Mincio River, where Sparafucile and his sister, Maddalena, live. By letting her see the Duke's faithlessness, Rigoletto hopes to gain his daughter's consent to his planned revenge. The Duke arrives in a soldier's uniform, laughs at the fickleness of women, and makes love to Maddalena. Rigoletto sends his distraught daughter to wait for him in Verona and then contracts with Sparafucile for the Duke's murder.

As a storm approaches, the Duke goes to sleep in an upstairs room of the inn. Maddalena pleads with her brother to spare the life of the handsome stranger as Gilda furtively returns outside. Sparafucile agrees to spare the Duke only if another victim can be found, and Gilda determines to sacrifice her own life. She enters the inn and is stabbed.

Rigoletto returns to claim the Duke's corpse, and Sparafucile gives him a sack with the body in it. Rigoletto exults in his revenge until he hears the Duke singing in the distance. Tearing open the sack, Rigoletto discovers his daughter. He is consumed in an agony of grief and despair, while Gilda asks forgiveness and promises that in Heaven she and her mother will pray for him. As she dies, Rigoletto utters a final heart-wrenching cry, "Ah, the curse!"

La Traviata

ACT I

At a glittering party in her Paris home, the beautiful demi-mondaine Violetta Valery is introduced to Alfredo Germont, a young man who has long been an admirer and who came to ask about her every day during her recent illness. Alfredo proposes a toast to beauty and joy, in which Violetta joins him. Suddenly overcome by a coughing spell, she sends the other guests into the next room to dance, but Alfredo remains behind. He confesses that he has loved her for a year; though she dismisses all thoughts of love, she gives him a camellia and tells him to return again when it has withered. After the guests depart, Violetta wonders whether Alfredo might be the man to bring true love into her life, but then insists that she must remain forever free.

ACT II

Scene 1: A Country House outside Paris

Violetta has given up her lavish life in Paris to live in idyllic tranquility in the country with Alfredo. From Violetta's maid, Alfredo learns that his lover is selling all her possessions in order to pay the debts the couple has incurred. He leaves at once for Paris, determined to settle the debts himself.

Violetta is expecting her lawyer, but is surprised by the arrival of Alfredo's father, Giorgio Germont. He upbraids Violetta for ruining his son, but is taken aback when she shows him a deed for the sale of her property. Violetta tells him that

Alfredo's love has redeemed her past, but Germont nonetheless begs her to leave his son. Alfredo's sister is engaged to be married; her fiancé's family will not permit the marriage if Alfredo's liaison with Violetta continues. Recognizing that she can never escape the implacable condemnation of society, Violetta agrees to sacrifice her own love for Germont's daughter.

Violetta is writing a letter to Alfredo when he returns, announcing that his father is on his way but that he is sure Germont will love Violetta when he meets her. Begging Alfredo to love her always, Violetta rushes out. A messenger soon arrives with her letter to Alfredo. Germont returns to comfort his son, and Alfredo, discovering that Violetta has left him, falls grief-stricken into his father's arms. Germont tries to convince Alfredo that he can find peace and happiness with his family, but his son hardly hears him. Finding Violetta's invitation to a party given by the courtesan Flora Bervoix, Alfredo rushes off to Paris, jealously assuming that Violetta has returned to her protector, the Baron Douphol.

Scene 2: A Salon in the Paris Home of Flora Bervoix

At Flora's party, Alfredo has good luck playing cards. Violetta arrives, escorted by Douphol, and Alfredo challenges the Baron to play. The Baron is soundly beaten, and the guests go in to dinner. Violetta returns, having sent word for Alfredo to meet her. Afraid of what the Baron might do, Violetta pleads with Alfredo to leave, but he refuses to depart without her. Unable to reveal the real reason for her refusal, Violetta claims to be in love with the Baron. Enraged, Alfredo summons the guests and denounces his faithless lover, throwing his gambling winnings in her face as payment for her sacrifices.

Germont enters just at that moment, in search of his son, and condemns Alfredo, who is stricken by remorse. Violetta collapses as the Baron challenges Alfredo to a duel.

ACT III

Violetta is dying of consumption, destitute and forgotten by most of her friends. The doctor reassures her that she will recover but confides to Violetta's faithful maid that her mistress has only a short time to live. Violetta sends her maid to distribute the last of her money to the poor. Alone, she reads a letter from Germont reporting that the duel took place and that the Baron was wounded. Alfredo was forced to flee the country, but Germont had told him of Violetta's sacrifice and promises that Alfredo will return to ask her forgiveness. Violetta realizes that he will arrive too late and prays for the mercy of Heaven.

Alfredo enters, and the lovers fall into each others arms. Alfredo promises to take Violetta far from Paris so she can regain her health. Violetta tries to rise and go to church with Alfredo but does not have the strength. Horrified, Alfredo sees that she is near death and sends her maid for the doctor. Germont enters to bestow his blessings on the lovers and is stricken by the devastation he has precipitated. Violetta gives Alfredo a locket, telling him that when he marries he must give it to his bride and tell her that someone in Heaven is praying for them both. For a moment her strength seems to return, and Violetta feels herself reborn. Then she falls back, dead.

Simon Boccanegra

In a square outside the palace of the noble Fiesco family in Genoa, Paolo, a leader of the plebeian party, determines to elect the corsair Simon Boccanegra as the new Doge. Simon is not interested in political power, but Paolo persuades him to accept the nomination. Simon is in love with Fiesco's daughter, Maria, and their affair has resulted in an illegitimate child; Fiesco still refuses, however, to consent to their marriage. Paolo reminds Simon that even Fiesco could not refuse his daughter to the new Doge, and Simon accepts his proposal. After Simon departs, Paolo summons the plebeians and convinces them to elect Simon.

Fiesco now emerges from his palace, mourning the death of his daughter and denouncing her seducer. Simon, unaware of Maria's death, returns to beg Fiesco's forgiveness, even offering his life in atonement; the old man is implacable. Peace between them is possible only if Simon returns Fiesco's granddaughter to him. Simon cannot comply. His daughter was being raised in secrecy on the shores of a foreign land. When Simon last visited, the old woman to whom she had been entrusted had died, and the child had vanished.

Fiesco departs, declaring that without the return of his granddaughter there can be no peace. Simon cautiously enters the palace to see Maria again, only to discover her corpse. Overcome by grief, Simon staggers from the palace as the populace fills the square, hailing him as the new Doge.

ACT I

Scene 1: A Garden of the Grimaldi Palace, 25 Years Later

Amelia Grimaldi and her lover, Gabriele Adorno, swear their eternal devotion. The imminent arrival of Doge Simon is announced, and Amelia asks Gabriele to arrange their wedding swiftly, since the Doge seeks to marry her to his favorite, Paolo. Gabriele is left alone with Amelia's guardian, Andrea—who, unbeknownst to Amelia, is really Fiesco, in hiding because of his plotting against the Doge—and asks for Amelia's hand in marriage.

Fiesco reveals that Amelia is not really a Grimaldi, but an orphan adopted by the family to impersonate the heiress; the real Amelia had died, and, with her brothers exiled, the Grimaldi fortune would otherwise have been confiscated by Simon. To forestall the Doge's greed, the family initiated the present deception. Gabriele is undaunted by Amelia's humble origins, and Fiesco blesses their union.

Simon meets Amelia and pardons her brothers. Touched by his generosity, she reveals that she is not really Amelia Grimaldi. As she describes the particulars of her childhood and the death of the old woman who cared for her, the hope dawns within Simon that Amelia is his lost daughter, Maria. When the truth is confirmed, the two embrace in joyful reunion.

Simon tells Paolo to abandon all hope of marriage to Amelia, but Paolo, undaunted, plots her abduction when the Doge departs.

Scene 2: The Council Chamber of the Doge's Palace

Presiding over an assembly of the Genovese Council, Simon is calling for peace with their neighbors when the uproar of a revolt is heard outside the palace. Believing Simon responsible for Amelia's abduction, Gabriele has raised a mob calling for the Doge's death, but Simon authoritatively faces down the insurrection. The mob then bursts into the Council chamber, dragging in Gabriele, who tries to assassinate the Doge. At that moment, Amelia arrives and relates how she gained her freedom. Plebeians and patricians in the Council blame each other for the abduction, and a brawl ensues.

With great majesty, Simon denounces this endless fratricidal strife, lamenting the devastation it has brought to Genoa, and calling for peace and love. He pardons Gabriele for his attempted assassination, then turns to Paolo. Simon knows that Paolo is responsible for Amelia's abduction, but rather than arrest him, the Doge calls down the curse of Heaven on whoever instigated this latest round of violence. Accepting Simon's challenge to repeat the oath, Paolo curses himself, then flees in horror from the chamber.

ACT II

Paolo enters the Doge's chambers in the palace, swearing revenge and putting poison in the Doge's water glass. Fiesco and Gabriele have been detained in the palace, and Paolo orders them brought to him. He tries to persuade Fiesco to kill Simon, but the old man proudly refuses to degrade himself. Paolo then tells Gabriele that Simon intends to seduce Amelia, leaving the tormented lover in the chambers to murder the Doge.

Amelia enters, but when confronted by Gabriele, she will say only that her love for Simon is pure and innocent. As Simon approaches, she hurries Gabriele out of sight onto a balcony. Amelia greets her father and reveals to him that she loves Gabriele. Simon is distraught, having found Gabriele's name on a list of those who plotted against him. Amelia begs for forgiveness, but at first Simon refuses. Finally, he begins to relent and promises a pardon if Gabriele will repent. He then asks the reluctant Amelia to leave him.

Alone, Simon is tormented by conflicting thoughts of revenge and forgiveness. Wearily he drinks from Paolo's poisoned glass and drifts to sleep. Gabriele prepares to stab him, but Amelia returns and intercedes. The Doge awakens to confront Gabriele, who declares that he will avenge his father, who fell at Simon's hand. Simon responds that in stealing his daughter, Gabriele has already achieved his revenge. Discovering that Amelia is Simon's daughter, Gabriele is stricken with remorse for his jealous rage and swears reconcilation with the Doge. Simon forgives his former enemy, and, as the sounds of revolt are again heard outside the palace, the two men join in new alliance.

ACT III

The revolt has been quelled, and Paolo is led away through the palace to his execution for instigating the tumult. He confesses to Fiesco that he poisoned the Doge, then hears in the distance the wedding chorus celebrating the union of Gabriele and Amelia. A captain announces to the city that Simon has ordered all the torches to be extinguished out of respect for the dead, then Simon enters. Consumed by Paolo's poison, Simon looks longingly out the window at the sea and thinks of the life that might have been. Fiesco emerges from concealment, confronting the Doge and announcing in a terrible voice that at long last he will have his revenge. Recognizing Fiesco, Simon is filled with joy, for he can now return the old man's granddaughter and gain his forgiveness. He reveals that Amelia is, in fact, Maria Boccanegra; Fiesco, who never suspected her true identity, is filled with remorse for his implacable hatred. Hearing the voice of Heaven in Simon's words of love and forgiveness, Fiesco embraces his old enemy in friendship and peace.

Fiesco tells Simon that he has been poisoned, but the Doge asks him to say nothing to Amelia. When she enters with Gabriele, Simon tells her that Fiesco is her grandfather and invokes the blessing of Heaven on the newlywed couple. Appointing Gabriele as the new Doge of Genoa, Simon turns for one final glimpse of the sea, dying with a final whisper, "Maria."

Otello

ACT I

A storm pounds Cyprus while the populace awaits the arrival of Otello, the Moorish general appointed by Venice as governor of the island. The storm abates, his ship docks, and Otello is greeted with joy by the crowd as he announces the defeat of the Turkish fleet.

Only Jago and Roderigo do not rejoice. Jago, Otello's ensign, is bitter at being passed over for promotion in favor of Cassio and determines to discredit his rival. He easily recruits the aid of Roderigo, a Venetian noble who is in love with Otello's wife, Desdemona, and readily believes that Cassio is another rival for her affections. Together the two ply Cassio with wine and provoke a drunken brawl.

Otello arrives to restore order, demanding to know from Jago what transpired. Jago disingenuously claims ignorance, and Otello strips Cassio of his rank. Left alone, Otello and Desdemona tenderly embrace, recalling their courtship and swearing their eternal love.

ACT II

In a room of the castle overlooking a garden, Jago urges Cassio to talk with Desdemona and ask her to intercede with Otello. As Cassio goes off to await her, Jago proclaims his blasphemous *Credo* to the audience: all humanity is debased and wicked; all virtue and nobility are merely deception.

As Cassio talks with Desdemona in the garden, Otello

enters. Jago mutters about Cassio's suspicious conduct and
wonders about his earlier relationship with Desdemona in
Venice. Having aroused Otello's suspicions, he warns the Moor
to beware of jealousy; Otello vows to have proof. Observing
Desdemona with the children of Cyprus in the garden, Otello
cannot believe her to be unfaithful. When she enters and
begins to plead Cassio's case, however, his suspicions are rekin-
dled. He complains of a headache, but when Desdemona tries
to bind his forehead, using the handkerchief that Otello had
given her as his first love token, he casts it aside. Jago's wife,
Emilia, who is Desdemona's lady-in-waiting, retrieves the
handkerchief, but Jago quickly snatches it from her.

Left alone with Jago, Otello is tormented by jealousy. He
turns with fury on his ensign, demanding proof of Desdemona's infidelity. Jago responds by relating how one night he
ostensibly overheard Cassio talking in his sleep and declaring
his love for Desdemona. Jago then tells the hapless Moor that
he saw Desdemona's handkerchief in Cassio's possession.
Otello explodes with jealous rage; he vows vengeance, and
Jago joins him in the oath.

ACT III

In the great hall of the castle, Jago tells Otello to conceal
himself and eavesdrop while Cassio talks about Desdemona.
Desdemona arrives to plead for Cassio. Beside himself, Otello
demands the handkerchief that he gave her and, when she is
unable to produce it, denounces her as a harlot.

Alone, Otello determines that Desdemona will confess and
die. Jago returns and is soon joined by Cassio, who has discovered the handkerchief that Jago planted in his room. Jago jokes

with Cassio about his mistress, Bianca, and admires the handkerchief, leading the concealed Otello to believe that they are
talking about Desdemona. As Cassio leaves, the arrival of the
Venetian ambassadors is announced. Otello, urged on by Jago,
plans to smother Desdemona in her bed.

The ambassadors bring orders recalling Otello to Venice
and appointing Cassio in his place; Jago fuels the ambassadors'
uneasiness about the Moor's strange behavior. At last, Otello
summons Desdemona and, having read the ambassadors'
order, casts her to the ground before the assembled company.
As the crowd is paralyzed with horror, Jago surreptitiously
urges Otello to kill Desdemona that very night and then convinces Roderigo to dispatch Cassio. Nearly senseless in his
frenzy, Otello orders the onlookers to leave him, cursing
Desdemona before falling unconscious. Alone, Jago mocks the
fallen hero.

ACT IV

In her room, the unhappy Desdemona prepares for bed.
She asks Emilia to lay out her bridal gown and see that she is
buried in it. She sings the Willow Song, a mournful ballad she
learned from one of her mother's maidservants who had been
abandoned by her lover. Bidding Emilia farewell, Desdemona
prays to the Blessed Virgin before going to bed. Otello enters
silently and extinguishes the torch illuminating the room. He
gazes at the sleeping Desdemona, then kisses her. She awakens, and he tries in vain to force a confession of her faithlessness. At last he smothers her.

Emilia enters, announcing that Cassio has killed Roderigo.
Finding Desdemona dying, Emilia tells Otello that he has been

deceived and reveals how Jago came into possession of the handkerchief. Cassio and the other Venetians confront Jago, who flees.

Otello stabs himself, falling on the body of his innocent wife, imploring with his last breath one final kiss.

Selected Bibliography

Texts and Scores

Anicet-Bourgeois, and Francis Cornu. *Nabuchodonosor.* Paris, 1836.

Dumas, Alexandre, fils. *Théâtre complet de Alexandre Dumas fils.* Paris, 1868.

Gutiérrez, Antonio Garcia. *Simón Bocanegra.* Ed. Luis F. Díaz Larios. Barcelona: Editorial Planeta, 1989.

Hugo, Victor. *Théâtre complet de Victor Hugo.* Ed. J.-J.Thierry and Josette Mélèze. 2 vols. Monaco: Éditions Gallimard, 1963.

Shakespeare, William. *The Riverside Shakespeare.* Ed. G. Blakemore Evans. Boston: Houghton Mifflin Company, 1974.

Verdi, Giuseppe. *Ernani.* Milan: G. Ricordi & C., 1984.

―――. *Macbeth.* Milan: G. Ricordi & C., 1973.

―――. *Nabucco.* Milan: G. Ricordi & C., 1975.

―――. *Otello.* Milan: G. Ricordi & C., 1969.

―――. *Rigoletto.* Ed. Martin Chusid. Chicago and Milan: University of Chicago Press and G. Ricordi & C., 1985.

―――. *Simon Boccanegra.* Milan: G. Ricordi & C., 1963.

―――. *La Traviata.* Milan: G. Ricordi & C., 1988.

Works Consulted

Abbiati, Franco. *Giuseppe Verdi.* 4 vols. Milan: G. Ricordi & C., 1959.

Adamson, Jane. *Othello as Tragedy: Some Problems of Judgment and Feeling.* London: Cambridge University Press, 1980.

Affron, Charles. *A Stage for Poets: Studies in the Theatre of Hugo and Musset.* Princeton: Princeton University Press, 1971.

Atti del congresso internazionale di studi verdiani 3d, Milan, 1972. Parma: Istituto di Studi Verdiani, 1974.

Atti del 1 congresso internazionale di studi verdiani, Venice, 1966. Parma: Istituto di Studi Verdiani, 1969.

Avant-Scène Opéra. (Macbeth) March–April 1982.

――――. (Nabucco) April 1986.

――――. (Otello) May–June 1976.

――――. (Rigoletto) September–October 1988.

――――. (Simon Boccanegra) January–February 1979.

――――. (La Traviata) April 1983.

Baldini, Gabriele. Abitare la battaglia: la storia di Giuseppe Verdi. Milan: Garzanti Editore, 1970.

Balthazar, Scott Leslie. "Evolving Conventions in Italian Serious Opera: Scene Structure in the Works of Rossini, Bellini, Donizetti, and Verdi, 1810–1850." Diss., University of Pennsylvania, 1985.

――――. "Music, Poetry, and Action in Ottocento Opera: The Principle of Concurrent Articulations." Opera Journal 22/2 (1989): 12–34.

Barbier, Patrick. La Vie quotidienne à l'Opéra au temps de Rossini et de Balzac, Paris/1800–1850. Paris: Hachette, 1987.

Basevi, Abramo. Studio sulle opere di Giuseppe Verdi. Florence, 1859.

Beghelli, Marco. "Per un nuovo approccio al teatro musicale: l'atto performativo come luogo dell'imitazione gestuale nella drammaturgia verdiana." Italica 64 (1987): 632–53.

Bellaigue, Camille. Review of Rigoletto by Giuseppe Verdi. Revue des deux mondes 68 (1885):696–704.

Berthier, Philippe, and Kurt Ringger, eds. Littérature et opéra. Grenoble: Presses Universitaires de Grenoble, 1987.

Bloom, Harold, ed. Modern Critical Interpretations: William Shakespeare's Othello. New York: Chelsea House Publishers, 1987.

Bollettino dell'Istituto di Studi Verdiani 3 (1969–82).

Bradley, A.C. Shakespearean Tragedy. 1904. Reprint, New York: St. Martin's Press, 1985.

Brockway, Wallace, and Herbert Weinstock. The World of Opera: The Story of Its Development and the Lore of Its Performance. London: Methuen & Co., Ltd., 1963.

Brown, John Russell, ed. *Focus on Macbeth.* London: Routledge & Kegan Paul, 1982.

Budden, Julian. *The Operas of Verdi.* 3 vols. New York: Oxford University Press, 1973.

———. "The Two Traviatas." *Proceedings of the Royal Musical Association* 99 (1972–73):43–66.

———. *Verdi.* New York: Vintage Books, 1987.

Busch, Hans, trans. and ed. *Verdi's Otello and Simon Boccanegra (revised version) in Letters and Documents.* 2 vols. Oxford: Clarendon Press, 1988.

Carlson, Marvin. "French Stage Composition from Hugo to Zola." *Educational Theatre Journal* 23 (1971):363–78.

———. *The French Stage in the Nineteenth Century.* Metuchen, New Jersey: The Scarecrow Press, Inc., 1972.

———. "*Hernani's* Revolt from the Tradition of French Stage Composition." *Theatre Survey* 13/1 (1972):1–27.

Chahine, Samia. *La Dramaturgie de Victor Hugo* (1816–1843). Paris: Éditions A.-G. Nizet, 1971.

Challis, Bennett. "The Technique of Operatic Acting." *Musical Quarterly* 13 (1927):630–45.

Chorley, Henry F. *Thirty Years' Musical Recollections.* Ed. Ernest Newman. New York: Alfred A. Knopf, 1926.

Clément, Catherine. *Opera, or the Undoing of Women.* Trans. Betsy Wing. Minneapolis: University of Minnesota Press, 1988.

Coe, Doug. "The Original Production Book for *Otello*: An Introduction." *19th Century Music* 2 (1978):148–58.

Cohen, H. Robert, and Marie-Odile Gigou. *Cent ans de mise en scène lyrique en France (env. 1830–1930).* New York: Pendragon Press, 1986.

———. "Notes et documents (la conservation de la tradition scénique sur la scène lyrique en France au XIXe siècle: les livrets de mise en scène et la Bibliothèque de l'Association de la Régie théâtrale." *Revue de musicologie* 64 (1978):253–67.

Conati, Marcello. *La Bottega della musica: Verdi e la Fenice.* Milan: Il Saggiatore, 1983.

Conrad, Peter. *Romantic Opera and Literary Form.* Berkeley: University of California Press, 1977.

Cooper, Barbara T. "Staging Hugo in 1985." *Romance Notes* 26 (1986):286–93.

Daniels, Robert D. "Portrait of a Villain." *Opera News* 38/14 (1974):24–25.

Descotes, Maurice. "Du drame à l'opéra: les transpositions lyriques du théâtre de Victor Hugo." *Revue de la société d'histoire du théâtre* 34 (1982):103–56.

Dilla, Geraldine P. "Music-Drama: An Art-Form in Four Dimensions." *Musical Quarterly* 10 (1924):492–99.

Dolmetson, C. Review of *Rigoletto* by Giuseppe Verdi. *Opera Canada* 27/4 (1986):37.

Donington, Robert. *Opera and Its Symbols*. New Haven: Yale University Press, 1991.

Draper, F.W.M. *The Rise and Fall of the French Romantic Drama: with Special Reference to the Influence of Shakespeare, Scott and Byron*. New York: E.P. Dutton & Company, n.d.

Eliot, T.S. *Murder in the Cathedral*. New York: Harcourt Brace Jovanovich, Publishers, 1935.

Elliott, G.R. *Dramatic Providence in Macbeth: A Study of Shakespeare's Tragic Theme of Humanity and Grace*. Princeton: Princeton University Press, 1958.

Ernani by Giuseppe Verdi. Manuscript promptbook [I]. Paris: Association des Régisseurs Théâtrales, n.d.

————. Manuscript promptbook [II]. Paris: Association des Régisseurs Théâtrales, n.d.

La Fenice. Milan: Nuove Edizioni, 1972.

Gatti, Carlo, ed. *L'Abbozzo del Rigoletto*. Milan: Edizione Fuori Commercio di Giuseppe Verdi, 1941.

————. *Il Teatro alla Scala nella storia e nell'arte (1778–1963)*. 2 vols. Milan: G. Ricordi & C., 1964.

————. *Verdi: The Man and His Music*. Trans. Elizabeth Abbott. New York: G.P. Putnam's Sons, 1955.

Gautier, Théophile. *Histoire de l'art dramatique en France depuis vingt-cinq ans*. 4 vols. Paris, 1858.

Glachant, Paul and Victor. *Essai critique sur le théâtre de Victor Hugo*. 2 vols. Paris: Hachette, 1902.

Godefroy, Vincent. *The Dramatic Genius of Verdi: Studies of Selected Operas*. 2 vols. New York: St. Martin's Press, 1975.

Granville-Barker, Harley. *More Prefaces to Shakespeare*. Ed. Edward M. Moore. Princeton: Princeton University Press, 1974.

Greenfield, Edward. Review of *Rigoletto* by Giuseppe Verdi. *High Fidelity/Musical America* 33/7 (1983):38–40.

Grout, Donald Jay. *A Short History of Opera*. 2d ed. New York: Columbia University Press, 1965.

Gundry, Inglis. "The Nature of Opera as a Composite Art." *Proceedings of the Royal Musical Association* 73 (1946–47):25–33.

Hepokoski, James A. *Giuseppe Verdi: Otello*. London: Cambridge University Press, 1987.

Héquet, G. Review of *Rigoletto* by Giuseppe Verdi. *L'Illustration, journal universel* 29 (1857):67.

Hogarth, George. *Memories of the Opera in Italy*. 2 vols. London, 1851.

Howarth, W.D. *Sublime and Grotesque: A Study of French Romantic Drama*. London: George G. Harrap & Co. Ltd., 1975.

Hussey, Dyneley. *Verdi*. London: J.M. Dent and Sons Ltd., 1963.

Hyman, Stanley Edgar. *Iago: Some Approaches to the Illusion of His Motivation*. New York: Atheneum, 1970.

Illustrated London News. Review of *Ernani* by Giuseppe Verdi. 15 March 1845:168.

———. Review of *Nino* by Giuseppe Verdi. 7 March 1846:162.

———. Review of *Nino* by Giuseppe Verdi. 12 April 1948:217.

———. Review of *Rigoletto* by Giuseppe Verdi. 22 May 1853:399.

———. Review of *Rigoletto* by Giuseppe Verdi. 5 June 1886:596.

Kestner, Joseph. "La Maledizione." *Opera News* 54/11 (1990):21–25.

Kimbell, David R.B. *Verdi in the Age of Italian Romanticism*. London: Cambridge University Press, 1981.

Knight, G. Wilson. *The Wheel of Fire: Interpretations of Shakespearean Tragedy with Three New Essays*. New York: Barnes and Noble, Inc., 1966.

Lindenberger, Herbert. *Opera: The Extravagant Art*. Ithaca: Cornell University Press, 1984.

Loewenberg, Alfred, comp. *Annals of Opera*. 2 vols. 3d ed. Totowa, New Jersey: Rowan and Littlefield, 1978.

Long, Michael. *Macbeth: Twayne's New Critical Editions to Shakespeare*. Boston: Twayne Publishers, 1989.

Lumley, Benjamin. *Reminiscences of the Opera*. London, 1864.

Martin, George. *Verdi: His Music, Life and Times.* New York: Dodd, Mead & Company, 1983.

Matthews, Brander. "The Conventions of the Music-Drama." *Musical Quarterly* 5 (1919):255–63.

―――. *French Dramatists of the Nineteenth Century.* 3d ed. New York: Benjamin Blom, 1901.

Medici, Mario, and Marcello Conati, eds. *Carteggio Verdi-Boito.* 2 vols. Parma: Istituto di Studi Verdiani, 1978.

Meisel, Martin. *Realizations: Narrative, Pictorial, and Theatrical Arts in Nineteenth-Century England.* Princeton: Princeton University Press, 1983.

Mila, Massimo. *L'Arte di Verdi.* Turin: Giulio Einaudi Editore, 1980.

―――. *Giuseppe Verdi.* Bari: Editori Laterza, 1958.

―――, ed. *Il Melodramma italiano dell'ottocento: studi e ricerche per Massimo Mila.* Turin: Giulio Einaudi Editore, 1977.

Miragoli, Livia. *Il Melodramma italiano nell'ottocento.* Rome: P. Maglione & C., 1924.

Moreen, Robert Anthony. "Integration of Text Forms and Musical Forms in Verdi's Early Opera." Diss., Princeton University, 1975.

Noske, Frits. "*Othello*: Drama through Structure." In *Essays on Music for Charles Warren Fox,* ed. Jerald C. Graue. Rochester: Eastman School of Music Press, 1979. Pp. 14–47.

Osborne, Charles. *The Complete Operas of Verdi.* New York: Da Capo Press, 1969.

―――. *Rigoletto: A Guide to the Opera.* London: Barrie & Jenkins, 1979.

Parker, R. "Levels of Motivic Definition in Verdi's *Ernani*." *19th Century Music* 6 (1982):141–50.

Pelz, Mary Ellis, and Gerald Fitzgerald, comps. *Metropolitan Opera Annals Third Supplement: 1966–76.* Clifton, New Jersey: James T. White & Company, 1978.

Pendell, William P. *Victor Hugo's Acted Dramas and the Contemporary Press.* Baltimore: The Johns Hopkins University Press, 1947.

Pintorno, Giuseppe, ed. *Le Prime: duecento anni di Teatro alla Scala.* Milan: Grafica Gutenberg Editrice, 1982.

Planche, Gustave. Review of *Le Roi s'amuse* by Victor Hugo. *Revue des deux mondes* 8 (1832):567–81.

Prod'homme, J.-G. "Lettere inédités de G. Verdi a Léon Escudier." *Rivista musicale italiana* 35 (1928):1+.

————. *L'Opéra (1669–1925).* Paris: Librairie Delagrave, 1925.

Revue des deux mondes. Review of *Nabucodonosor* by Giuseppe Verdi. 12 (1845):523–26.

Ricordi, Gulio, ed. *Disposizione scenica per l'opera Otello.* Milan, 1887.

Rigoletto by Giuseppe Verdi. Manuscript promptbook [I].Paris: Association des Régisseurs Théâtrales, n.d.

————. Manuscript promptbook [II]. Paris: Association des Régisseurs Théâtrales, n.d.

————. Manuscript promptbook [III]. Paris: Association des Régisseurs Théâtrales, n.d.

————. Manuscript promptbook [IV]. Paris: Association des Régisseurs Théâtrales, n.d.

Rinaldi, Mario. *Felice Romani: dal melodramma classico al melodramma romantico.* Rome: Edizioni di Santis, 1965.

————. *Le Opere più note di Giuseppe Verdi.* Florence: Leo S. Alschki, 1986.

Rolandi, Ulderico. *Il Libretto per musica attraverso i tempi.* Rome: Edizioni dell'Ateneo, 1951.

Roncaglia, Gino. "L'Abbozzo del Rigoletto di Verdi." *Rivista musicale italiana* 48 (1946):112–29.

Rosen, David, and Andrew Porter, eds. *Verdi's Macbeth: A Sourcebook.* New York: W. W. Norton & Company, 1984.

Rosenberg, Marvin. *The Masks of Macbeth.* Berkeley: University of California Press, 1978.

————. *The Masks of Othello.* Berkeley: University of California Press, 1961.

Rosenthal, Harold. Review of *Rigoletto* by Giuseppe Verdi. *Opera* 33 (1982):1197–1200.

————. *Two Centuries of Opera at Covent Garden.* London: Putnam, 1958.

Sadie, Stanley. Review of *Rigoletto* by Giuseppe Verdi. *Musical Times* 123 (1982):771.

Schmidgall, Gary. *Literature as Opera.* New York: Oxford University Press, 1977.

————. *Shakespeare and Opera.* New York: Oxford University Press, 1990.

Seltsam, William H., comp. *Metropolitan Opera Annals: A Chronicle of Artists and Performances.* New York: The H.W. Wilson Company, 1947.

――――. *Metropolitan Opera Annals (First Supplement: 1947–57): A Chronicle of Artists and Performances.* New York: The H.W. Wilson Company, 1957.

――――. *Metropolitan Opera Annals (Second Supplement: 1957–1966):* A Chronicle of Artists and Performances. New York: The H.W. Wilson Company, 1968.

Shaw, Bernard. *Shaw's Music: The Complete Musical Criticism in Three Volumes.* Ed. Dan H. Laurence. 3 vols. New York: Dodd, Mead & Company, 1981.

Smith, Patrick J. *The Tenth Muse: A Historical Study of the Opera Libretto.* New York: Schirmer Books, 1975.

Soffredini, A. *Le Opere di Verdi: studio critico analitico.* Milan: Carlo Aliprandi, 1901.

Stocker, Leonard. "Hugo's *Hernani* and Verdi's *Ernani.*" *Southern Quarterly* 8 (1970):357–81.

Studi verdiani. 3 vols. Parma: Istituto di Studi Verdiani, 1985.

Styan, J.L. *Shakespeare's Stagecraft.* London: Cambridge University Press, 1967.

Sutcliffe, J.H. Review of *Rigoletto* by Giuseppe Verdi. *Opera* 37 (1986):1073–75.

Tintori, Gianpiero, ed. *La Scala.* Milan: Nuove Edizioni Milano, 1966.

Tomlinson, Gary. "Donizetti, Verdi, and Hugo's Romantic Drama." *Verdi Newsletter* 11 (1983):24–25.

Torchi, L. "L'Opera di Giuseppe Verdi e i suoi caratteri principali." *Rivista musicale italiana* 8 (1901):279–325.

Ubersfeld, Anne. *Le Roi et le buffon: étude sur le théâtre de Hugo de 1830 à 1839.* Paris: Librairie José Corti, 1974.

Verdi, Giuseppe. I *Copialettere di Giuseppe Verdi.* Ed. Gaetano Cesari and Alessandro Luzio. Milan: Forni Editore Bologna, 1913.

――――. *Letters of Giuseppe Verdi.* Ed. and trans. Charles Osborne. London: Victor Gollancz Ltd., 1971.

――――. *Re Lear e Ballo in Maschera: Lettere di Giuseppe Verdi ad Antonio Somma.* Ed. Alessandro Pascolato. Citta di Castello: Casa Editrice S. Lapi, 1913.

————. *Verdi: The Man in His Letters*. Ed. Franz Werfel and Paul Stefan; trans. Edward Downes. New York: L.B. Fischer, 1942.

Verdi e la Fenice: Ernani, Attila, Rigoletto, Traviata, Simon Boccanegra. Venice: Electra Editrice, 1980.

Verdi Newsletter 1–15 (1976–87).

————. 9–10 (1981–82).

Visetti, Albert. "Tendencies of the Operatic Stage in the Nineteenth Century." *Proceedings of the Musical Association* 22 (1896):141–51.

Weaver, William, trans. *Seven Verdi Librettos*. New York: W.W. Norton & Company Inc., 1963.

————, ed. *Verdi: A Documentary Study*. New York: Thames and Hudson, n.d.

————, and Martin Chusid, eds. *The Verdi Companion*. New York: W.W. Norton & Company, 1979.

Weiss, Piero. "Verdi and the Fusion of Genres." *Journal of the American Musicological Society* 35 (1982):138–56.

Williams, Gordon. *Macbeth: Text and Performance*. London: Macmillan Publishers Ltd., 1985.

Wren, Keith. *Hernani and Ruy Blas*. London: Grant & Cutler Ltd., 1982.

Notes

Introduction

1. See Victor Hugo, Préface, *Cromwell*, in *Théâtre complet de Victor Hugo*, I:409–54.

2. Exceptions may, of course, be found. Manfredo, in Mercadante's *Il Giuramento*, for instance, is given an extended *scena* revealing great psychological complexity: "Alla pace degli eletti." But such moments are infrequent, and, even here, only highlight Manfredo's rather stock delineation in the rest of the opera.

3. G.B. Shaw was clearly dismayed by this innovation. Noting that healthy vocal writing requires the *tessitura* to remain in the middle of the voice, he conceded that the middle of the voice was often not the most beautiful or powerful part of a singer's register. "There is, therefore, a constant temptation to composers to use the upper fifth of the voice almost exclusively; and this is exactly what Verdi did without remorse. He practically treated that upper fifth as the whole voice, and pitched his melodies in the middle of it instead of in the middle of the entire compass.... The upshot of that, except in the case of abnormally pitched voices, was displacement, fatigue, intolerable strain, shattering *tremolo*, and finally, not, as could have been wished, total annihilation, but the development of an unnatural trick of making an atrociously disagreeable noise and inflicting it on the public as Italian singing." *Shaw's Music* III:580–81.

4. George Martin speculates that Verdi's predilection for the baritone voice may have sprung from his childhood in the male-dominated farming village of Busseto, where he would be surrounded almost exclusively by baritonal sound: "All around him, on the street and in Barezzi's store, he would have heard the lower tone to an extent impossible for a city child whose father goes away to work and

who spends almost the entire day among the piping voices of other children or women." *Verdi: His Life, Music and Times,* 188.

5. Among the contemporary critics evidencing a more interdisciplinary perspective are Julian Budden, *The Operas of Verdi;* Massimo Mila, *L'Arte di Verdi;* David R.B. Kimbell, *Verdi in the Age of Italian Romanticism;* and Gary Schmidgall, *Shakespeare and Opera.*

6. Shaw's parody of this distinguished critical school has become almost legendary: "How succulent this is; and how full of Mesopotamian words like 'the dominant of D minor'! I will now, ladies and gentlemen, give you my celebrated 'analysis' of Hamlet's soliloquy on suicide, in the same scientific style. 'Shakespear, dispensing with the customary exordium, announces his subject at once in the infinitive, in which mood it is presently repeated after a short connecting passage in which, brief as it is, we recognize the alternative and negative forms on which so much of the significance of repetition depends. Here we reach a colon; and a pointed pository phrase, in which the accent falls decisively on the relative pronoun, brings us to the first full stop.'

"I break off here, because, to confess the truth, my grammar is giving out. But I want to know whether it is just that a literary critic should be forbidden to make his living in this way on pain of being interviewed by two doctors and a magistrate, and haled off to Bedlam forthwith; whilst the more a musical critic does it, the deeper the veneration he inspires." *Shaw's Music* II:898–99.

7. See, for example, Robert Donington, *Opera and Its Symbols: The Unity of Words, Music, and Staging;* Catherine Clément, *Opera, or the Undoing of Women,* trans. Betsy Wing; or Herbert Lindenberger, *Opera: The Extravagant Art.*

8. In considering the totality of text, music, and staging in the portrayal of character, the present discussion will use each opera's original source play as an interpretive touchstone to highlight significant points of comparison and contrast, provide a descriptive analysis of Verdi's use of music in characterization, and examine such production resources as authorial correspondence, nineteenth-century reviews, and period promptbooks.

9. The term "metatheatrical" denotes works manifesting a self-conscious theatricality, a playful awareness of their own status as theatrical performance.

10. A particularly rich source of nineteenth-century staging information is found in the holdings of the Bibliothèque Historique de la Ville de Paris. See H. Robert Cohen and Marie-Odile Gigou, *Cent ans de mise en scène lyrique en France (env. 1830–1930)*; and H. Robert Cohen, "Livrets de mise en scène, Annotated Scores and Annotated Libretti in Two Parisian Collections," *Studi Verdiani* 3:11–44.

11. Representative reviews of this production include J.H. Sutcliffe, *Opera* 37 (1986):1073–75, and C. Dolmetson, *Opera Canada* 27/4 (1986):37.

12. Representative reviews of this production include Stanley Sadie, *Musical Times* 123 (1982):771; Harold Rosenthal, *Opera* 33 (1982):1197–1200; and Edward Greenfield, *High Fidelity/Musical America* 33/7 (1983):38–40.

13. Victor Hugo, Préface, *Marie Tudor*, in *Théâtre complet de Victor Hugo*, II:414.

Nabucco

1. *Illustrated London News*, 1 April 1848, 12–13:217.

2. 22 April 1853, in *Re Lear e Ballo in Maschera: Lettere di Giuseppe Verdi ad Antonio Somma*, 46. Verdi wrote, "Io rifiuterei oggi di scrivere soggetti sul genere del *Nabucco.* . . . Presentano punti di scena interessantissimi, ma senza varietà. È una corda sola, elevata se volete, ma pur sempre la stessa. E per spiegarmi meglio: il poema del Tasso sarà forse migliore, ma io preferisco mille e mille volte Ariosto. Per l'istessa ragione preferisco Shakespeare a tutti i drammatici, senza eccettuarne i Greci." (Today I would refuse to set subjects in the genre of *Nabucco.* . . . They offer moments of greatest theatrical interest, but without variety. There is only a single chord, elevated if you like, but always the same. To explain myself more clearly: the poetry of Tasso may be better, but I prefer a thousand thousand times Ariosto. For the same reason I prefer Shakespeare to all other dramatists, not excepting the Greeks.)

3. Such dramaturgical limitations, in turn, defy even the most accomplished of interpreters. Hence, Verdi's dissatisfaction despite the performance of baritone Giorgio Ronconi, whose creation of the role of Nabucco at La Scala received great critical acclaim: "Giorgio

Ronconi è sempre l'attore più vero ed il cantante più finito che ora ci è dato intendere. Nabuco [*sic*] non poteva trovar sulle scene un artista che lo rappresentasse con più d'intelligenza, e più di valore." (Giorgio Ronconi is still the most truthful actor and the most consummate singer we can hear today. Nabucco could not be represented on the stage by an artist of more intelligence and merit.) *Figaro*, 10 March 1842, in Pintorno, 36.

4. Verdi's account of how he compelled Solera to write a prophecy for Zaccaria in place of the librettist's proposed duet for Ismaele and Fenena is reproduced by Charles Osborne in *The Complete Operas of Verdi*, 49.

5. *Gazzetta Musicale di Milano*, 13 March 1842, in Pintorno, 37.

6. Julian Budden offers another perspective on the relationship of opera and play, as well as a detailed discussion of *Nabucco*'s connection with the *bel canto* tradition in *The Operas of Verdi* I:89–112.

7. *Nabuchodonosor*, 7. Hereafter, page numbers are cited in parentheses after the quotation.

8. *Nabucco*, 58. Hereafter, page numbers are cited in parentheses after the quotation.

9. In the play, by contrast, Nabuchodonosor replaces the crown on Phénenna. The staging of the play certainly highlights the king's defense of his child, but it lacks the subtler visual suggestion of Nabucco's shifting perception of his own power. The stage directions read, "NABUCHODONOSOR, qui s'est fait jouer au milieu du désordre, s'élance et se dresse entre Abigaïl et Phénenna, et crie à la première d'une voix tonnante, en mettant la main sur la coronne encore au front de Phénenna, 'Viens donc la prendre'" (14; Nabuchodonosor bursts forth from the midst of the disorder, places himself between Abigaïl and Phénenna, and cries to the first with a thunderous voice while putting his hand on the crown which rests again on Phénenna's head, "Now come take it").

10. Compare the psychological subtlety of this *scena* with the same moment in the play, where Nabuchodonosor's thoughts never progress beyond initial panic and defiance: "Étouffez-moi dans vos bras!.. écrasez-moi sous vos pieds... mais non... non... je ne peux pas mourir... je suis dieu... dieu" (22; Smother me in your arms! Crush me beneath your feet... but no... no... I cannot die... I am God, God).

11. It is interesting to note that this phrase also contains the melodic germ that Verdi would more fully develop in Germont's "Pura siccome un angelo" in the second act of *La Traviata*. Again, a father tries to give voice to a love that surpasses his capacity for articulate expression as he thinks of his daughter's happiness: "or si ricusa al vincolo che lieti, lieti ne rendeva" (95; [the young man] now will refuse the bond that made them both so happy).

12. A contemporary critic noted, "Se trouve face à face avec l'usurpatrice; ce roi, dis-je, me rappelle involontairement le vieux Lear, comme Abigaille me fait songer à ses filles." (Finding himself face to face with the usurper, this king, I say, involuntarily recalls to my mind the old Lear, just as Abigaille makes me think of his daughters.) *Revue des deux mondes* 12(1845):532.

13. The *Illustrated London News*, reviewing a production of the opera given under the title *Nino*, noted, "The character of Nino is remarkably suited to Fornasari, to whom the higher style of tragic parts is always well adapted. The scene of the imbecility and weakness of the proud Monarch was beautifully and pathetically rendered by this great artist. His haggard appearance, his tottering gait, his fallen pride—all were impersonated by him with admirable dramatic feeling." 7 March 1846:162.

14. Note, by contrast, Abigaille's contemptuous aside from the third act, "Assai... più vale il soglio che un genitor" (181; A throne is worth much more than a father).

15. By rights, the opera, like the play, should have ended on Nabucco's note of joyful affirmation. Instead, Abigaille is brought back on stage for a final *scena* of repentance before her death. It is a dramatic anomaly, an anticlimactic bit of melodrama that diffuses the focus on Nabucco's spiritual renewal. Significantly, this final scene was often omitted from nineteenth-century performances and, as Julian Budden points out, Verdi himself seems to have known about, and even condoned, this practice (112).

Ernani

1. Letter to Mocenigo, 5 September 1843, in Conati, 74–75.

2. *Illustrated London News*, 15 March 1845:168. This kind of insight makes all the more ironic the view of a more modern critic,

George Martin, who opines, "Within this general problem of operatic form, Verdi had some more personal difficulties, such as his inability to characterize his men and Elvira. Except for range and agility, the arias would almost be interchangeable between all four lovers." *Verdi: His Music, Life and Times,* 132.

3. *Hernani,* in *Théâtre complet de Victor Hugo,* I:1167. Hereafter, page numbers are cited in parentheses after the quotation.

4. 10 October 1843, in Conati, 94–95.

5. *Ernani,* 47. Hereafter, page numbers are cited in parentheses after the quotation.

6. Two nineteenth-century Paris stagings of this ensemble are particularly interesting in the relative importance they assign to the various principals. The promptbooks of both productions emphasize Carlo and Ernani by positioning them close to the center of the conventional downstage line of singers, while Elvira and Silva are pushed out to the edges. Promptbook [II] lists the order from stage right to stage left as follows: Giovanna, Elvira, Ernani, Carlo, Silva (a step further upstage than the others), and Riccardo (5). The inclusion of the *comprimari* in the line-up diffuses the focus on the principal characters but also highlights the distinctly secondary status of Silva, who is banished upstage. Promptbook [I] shows the *comprimari* upstage and the principals arrayed as follows: Silva, Carlo, Ernani, Elvira. In this staging, however, Carlo is given even more prominence by his blocking just prior to this ensemble: "Charles passe devant [Sylva] et gagne à droite pour dire à Ernani: nous nous verrons. Sylva qui a pris le No. 1 jette les yeux sur Ernani et dit: cet homme. En disant: est à moi Charles pose la main sur l'épaule droite d'Ernani, puis il regagne vers la gauche. Le grand ensemble commence et finit sans autre mouvement de scène." (I:11–12; Carlo crosses below Silva to the right to say to Ernani: "we will see." Silva, who moved to the left, casts his eyes on Ernani and says: "that man." While saying: "he is with me," Carlo puts his hand on Ernani's right shoulder, then moves left again. The ensemble begins and finishes without other movement.)

7. Shaw called this scene "the classic opportunity for lyric actors of the Italian school" and went on to compare Hugo's original with the operatic adaptation: "In the play Charles is sublime in feeling, but somewhat tedious in expression. In the opera he is equally sublime in feeling, but concise, grand, and touching in expression,

thereby proving that the chief glory of Victor Hugo as a stage poet
was to have provided libretti for Verdi." *Shaw's Music* II:724.

8. The Paris promptbooks both leave this scene in the hands of
the individual performer, noting only, "Charles seul" (I:25; Carlo
alone).

9. Carlo's heightened stature is clear in the final tableau of the
Paris staging, where "Elvire et Ernani se jettent aux genoux de
Charles" (I:32; Elvira and Ernani throw themselves down at Charles'
knees).

10. Promptbook [II]:20.

Macbeth

1. *Macbeth* premiered in Florence in 1847; it was later revised
into its final form for production in Paris in 1865. This discussion will
consider the revised version, but further analysis of Verdi's musical
development from 1847 to 1865 may be found in Julian Budden, *The
Operas of Verdi* I:268–312.

2. "The beautiful and terrible drama by Shakespeare has been
disfigured, lacerated, dislocated, shattered by an Italian librettist, il
signor Piave." Joseph d'Ortigue, *Journal des Débats*, 29 April 1865,
quoted in Rosen and Porter, *Verdi's Macbeth: A Sourcebook*, 409.

3. Letter to Tito Ricordi, 11 April 1857, in *I Coppialettere*, 444.

4. Letter from Muzio to Barezzi, 27 August 1846, in Rosen and
Porter, 7.

5. Letter to Varesi, 7 January 1847, ibid., 30.

6. Letter to Piave, 22 September 1846, in Abbiati I:645

7. Letter to Escudier, 28 April 1865, *Rivista musicale italiana* 35
(1928):187.

8. T.S. Eliot, *Murder in the Cathedral*, 25.

9. *Macbeth*, 17. Hereafter, page numbers are cited in parentheses
after the quotation.

Shakespeare's Lady Macbeth makes clear when she sees her husband that the murder of Duncan is something that has been discussed
before:

> What beast was't then
> That made you break this enterprise to me?

When you durst do it, then were you a man;
And to be more than what you were, you would
Be so much more the man. Nor time, nor place,
Did then adhere, and yet you would make both:
They have made themselves, and that their fitness now
Does unmake you.
[*Macbeth*, in *The Riverside Shakespeare*, I.vii.47–54. Hereafter, line numbers are cited in parentheses after the quotation.]

In the opera, this reference is omitted, and yet the murder seems so well understood between Macbeth and his wife that the sense of earlier discussion is retained.

10. As Michael Long notes, "Early on he hopes that chance may crown him, 'without my stir,' but he soon realises that it will not. He must stir, and act, and thus confront the fatality of individual deeds." *Macbeth*, 31–32.

11. The first Lady Macbeth, Marianna Barbieri-Nini, recalled rehearsing the duet "'Fatal mia donna" 150 times, "so that it would be closer to *speech* than to *singing*, the Maestro would say. Now listen to this. On the evening of the final rehearsal, with the theatre full, Verdi insisted that even the soloists should be in costume, and when he set his mind on something, woe if you opposed him! And so we were dressed and ready, the orchestra in place, the chorus on stage, when Verdi made a sign to me and Varesi, and called us backstage: he asked us—as a favor to him—to go with him into the foyer and rehearse that damned duet again at the piano." Rosen and Porter, 51.

12. Letter to Varesi, 7 January 1847, ibid., 31.

13. Verdi described his staging of this scene at the Florence première in 1847: "I had Banquo appear (with a large wound on his forehead) through a trapdoor from underground, precisely in Macbeth's place. He did not move, but only raised his head at the proper moment. It was terrifying." Ibid., 90.

14. Verdi himself suggested the staging of this scene in a letter to Salvatore Cammarano: "The stage is extremely dark. In the third act, the apparitions of the kings (I've seen it done in London) must take place behind an opening in the scenery, with a fine *ashen* veil in front of it. The *kings* should not be puppets, but eight men of flesh and blood. The floor over which they pass must resemble a mound,

and they must be seen clearly to ascend and descend. The scene must be completely dark, especially when the cauldron disappears, and lighted only where the *kings* pass. The music beneath the stage must be reinforced (for the large San Carlo Theatre), but be sure there are neither trumpets nor trombones. The sound must seem distant and muted, and must therefore be composed of bass clarinets, bassoons, contrabassoons, and nothing else." Ibid., 67.

15. This faint is faithful to Rusconi's Italian translation of Shakespeare's play, if not to the original English.

16. Letter to Escudier, 23 January 1865, in *I Coppialettere*, 452.

17. Kimbell, 546.

Rigoletto

1. Letter to Piave, 28 April 1850, in Conati, 197.

2. Letter from Verdi to Piave, 8 May 1850, in Conati, 198.

3. Nineteenth-century critics emphasized the power of *Rigoletto* as a vehicle for great singing actors. One reviewer of the La Scala première of the work declared, "È certo che se Verdi in questa opera si elevò all'altezza dei più grandi maestri, Corsi raggiunse quella dei più grandi attori drammatici." (It is certain that if Verdi elevates himself in this opera to the heights of the greatest composers, Corsi attains that of the greatest dramatic actors.) *Gazzetta Ufficiale di Milano,* 19 January 1853, quoted in Pintorno, 51.

The *Illustrated London News* noted, "Signor D'Andrade's performance as Rigoletto was also highly successful alike in its vocal and its dramatic aspects. He possesses a sympathetic baritone voice, his phrasing is highly artistic, and his impersonation of the unhappy Court jester was throughout forcible without being extravagant or grotesque." 5 June 1886:596.

Even Shaw, while deploring the general lack of attention to dramatic truth in much opera of the late nineteenth century, applauded the French baritone Victor Maurel for his Rigoletto: "If I were to say that Maurel is a great actor among opera singers, he might well retort 'Thank you for nothing: in the country of the blind the one-eyed is king.' So I will put it in this way—that his Rigoletto is as good a piece of acting as Edwin Booth's Triboulet; whilst the impression it makes is deeper, and the pleasure it gives greater, by just so much as Verdi is a greater man than Tom Taylor, which is saying a good deal." *Shaw's Music* II:205–206.

4. Letter to Presidente Marzari, 14 December 1850, in Conati, 233.

5. Gustave Planche, *Revue des deux mondes* 8 (1832):568.

6. *Le Roi s'amuse*, in *Théâtre complet de Victor Hugo*, I:1358. Hereafter, page numbers are cited in parentheses after the quotation.

7. *Rigoletto*, 10. Hereafter, page numbers are cited in parentheses after the quotation.

8. The promptbook from a nineteenth-century Paris production of the opera indicates a heightening of this effect: "[Monterone] étend le bras vers Rigoletto qui épouvanté courbe le tête et se réfugie à l'extreme droite" (Monterone extends his arm toward Rigoletto, who, terror-stricken, bows his head and takes refuge at the extreme right). Manuscript Promptbook [I], 9.

9. Préface, *Le Roi s'amuse*, 1326.

10. The kidnapping of Rigoletto's daughter, Gilda, cannot be construed as part of the curse, for the courtiers set this plan in motion long before Monterone makes his appearance.

11. It is interesting to contrast Hugo's explanation of Triboulet's behavior with the perceptions voiced by the jester in the play itself. In his later preface, Hugo declared, "Triboulet est difforme, Triboulet est malade, Triboulet est bouffon de cour; triple misère qui le rend méchant" (1326; Triboulet is deformed, Triboulet is sick, Triboulet is a jester; triple misery that makes him wicked). In his own monologue, however, Triboulet places the blame on the dehumanizing treatment of the court (1381).

12. The reviewer for the *Illustrated London News* emphasized the dramatic potential of this scene: "These dramatic situations supply a subject for musical illustration of which Verdi has forcibly availed himself in many points, and they have also given to Ronconi the opportunity of displaying his varied comic and tragic powers.... In fact, great as was the histrionic genius of Ronconi admitted to be, his 'Rigoletto' has combined displays of comedy and tragedy that can only recall the well-known picture of Garrick between Thalia and Melpomene. Let us instance the scene in the Ducal Palace, in the second act, in which Rigoletto strives to smile with the courtiers, whilst

his heart is breaking at the abduction of his child—an abduction in which he himself had been made innocently to assist. The expression of Ronconi's face in this scene—one half of the face that of the court-jester, the other half that of the bereaved father—can never be forgotten. To follow this great actor and singer throughout his wonderful delineation would form an essay of itself, and within these limits but a bare reference to the opera at large can be afforded." 22 May 1853:399.

13. The Paris promptbook [I] indicates a staging that emphasizes this dramatic conflict, for Gilda restrains Rigoletto from departing after his first verse and then at the end of the duet "se jette aux genoux de son père" (34; she throws herself at her father's knees).

14. The nineteenth-century suppression of this final duet is dramatically indefensible. In 1894 Shaw noted, "In *Rigoletto* the final duet was restored. As far as I know, it has never been done on the stage since its excision immediately after the opera was first produced." *Shaw's Music* III:246.

15. Critics have often discussed the dramatic, musical, and structural parallels between Verdi's *Rigoletto* and Donizetti's earlier Hugo adaptation, *Lucrezia Borgia* (revised 1840). The similarity in the dramatic vision of the two works is perhaps exemplified in the climactic final scenes of the operas. Lucrezia and Rigoletto find their attempts at self-affirmation bring about the destruction of the children whose love could have redeemed their lives of misery and the contempt of the world; and their last words are both haunting cries of inarticulate despair, Rigoletto's "la maledizione" echoing the collapsing phrase of Lucrezia's desolate "è spento."

La Traviata

1. Kimbell, 662.
2. 23 May 1857:496.
3. The details of this system of values are firmly grounded in the social milieu of the mid-nineteenth century, and it is certainly no credit to the production practices at the time of the opera's première that *La Traviata* was first performed in anomalous eighteenth-century costumes. Despite Verdi's vehement objections, the management of

La Fenice insisted on setting the opera in 1700, ostensibly to avoid public outrage over the subject matter, and this practice continued throughout the nineteenth century.

As late as 1891, Shaw archly noted the continuation of anomalous costuming and its detrimental effect on the opera: "Maurel is courageous in matters of costume: his Holbein dress as Valentin, his mouse-colored Mephistopheles, his stupendous helmet in Lohengrin . . . had proved him ready for any sacrifice of tradition to accuracy. I fully expected to see Germont enter fearlessly in frock-coat, tall hat, and primrose gloves with three black braids down the back. Judge of my disappointment when he marched forward in a magnificent Vandyke costume, without even an umbrella to save appearances. I knew then that he wanted, not to play Germont, but to sing *Di Provenza*. However, to do him justice, he did not treat the part with utter frivolity. He came in rudely with his hat on; and when he found that Violetta has a noble soul, he took his hat off, like a gentleman, and put it on a chair. I instantly foresaw that Albani, when next overcome by emotion, would sit on it. So breathless became my anticipation that I could hardly attend to the intervening duet. At last she did sit on it; and never would that hat have graced Maurel's temples again if it had been historically accurate. This, then, I presume, is the explanation of the anachronism on Maurel's part. Albani must have refused to give up the business of sitting on Germont's hat, thereby forcing him to adopt one that would bend but not break under an exceptional pressure of circumstances. But the effect on Maurel was finally disastrous." *Shaw's Music* II:326–27.

4. *La Traviata*, 91. Hereafter, page numbers are cited in parentheses after the quotation.

5. *La Dame aux camélias* in *Théâtre complet de Alexandre Dumas fils*, 125. Hereafter, page numbers are cited in parentheses after the quotation.

6. For further discussion of Verdi's revisions here and throughout the score after the 1853 première, see also Budden, "The Two Traviatas."

7. Interestingly, Verdi himself was to reveal his own personal sense of the inadequacy of such admonitions in a later letter to Clara Maffei after her husband's death. On 11 October 1883, he wrote: "Non vi sono parole che possano recar conforto a questa sorte di sventure. Ed io non vi dirò la sola stupida parola 'coraggio': parola che

ha sempre eccitata la mia ira quando diretta a me. Ci vuol altro!"
(There are no words that can bring comfort to this kind of misfor-
tune. And I will not say to you that one stupid word "courage": a
word that has always aroused my anger when directed at me. One
wants something else.) *I Copialettere,* 503.

    8. See, in contrast, Kimbell, 422.

    9. See also Budden, *The Operas of Verdi* II:148.

    10. See also Kimbell, 669.

Simon Boccanegra

    1. *Simon Boccanegra* premiered at the Teatro la Fenice in 1857
and was later revised for La Scala in 1881. This discussion will consider the definitive, revised version, but Julian Budden offers a
detailed comparison of the 1857 and 1881 scores in *The Operas of Verdi*
II:243–334.

    2. Busch II:666–67.

    3. Letter from Verdi to Boito, 11 December 1880, in *I
Copialettere,* 316.

    4. Letter to Giulio Ricordi, 20 November 1880, in Abbiati
IV:132.

    5. Letter to Giulio Ricordi, 2 December 1880, ibid.,137.

    6 Filippo Filippi found in Victor Maurel just such a singing actor:
"the first honours—this must be said and not disguised—belong to the
protagonist, the eminent baritone Maurel. He has revealed himself
already as a great singer and actor in *Ernani,* but in *Boccanegra* he is even
greater, perfect, and I dare say sublime. I would not know whether to
give more praise to the most refined, expressive singer in him, who
places so much emphasis on his phrases, or to the actor who embodies
himself in the character of the loyal, chivalrous, patriotic, generous,
passionate Doge, being all love and abnegation." Busch II:671.

    7. As Verdi noted in a letter to Maria Waldmann, dated 5 April
1881, "You would have heard ugly music, but a good performance and
a superb singing actor in the part of Simone (Maurel)!" Busch I:98.

    8. Eliot, 86.

    9. The *Disposizione scenica* for the La Scala *Simon* reinforces this
sense of Paolo as the driving force in the scene, indicating, "PAOLO

approaches him again to ask, 'Ti tenta ducal corona?' Upon BOCCA-
NEGRA's refusal, he gets even closer and whispers persuasively into his
ear, 'E Maria?'" (Does the Doge's crown tempt you?) Busch II:431.

10. *Simon Boccanegra*, 6. Hereafter, page numbers are cited in
parentheses after the quotation.

11. The only other explanation would be the implausible
assumption that his daughter's fate was witnessed by a neighbor who
dutifully reported to Simon but failed to take any steps to assist or
shelter the helpless child.

12. The *Disposizione* notes, "he appears pale, terrified, his hands
on his face, frightened by a terrible, horrible vision, and staggers to
centre-stage." Busch II:436.

13. This act of clemency is dramatically significant, not only for
foreshadowing the Doge's great monologue, "Plebe! Patrizi!" (131) in
the Council scene, but also for undercutting Fiesco's earlier assertions
of Simon's greed. Fiesco confesses to Gabriele that Amelia is not a
Grimaldi, but an orphan adopted by the family to impersonate the
heiress. The real Amelia has died, and, with her brothers exiled, the
Grimaldi fortune would otherwise have been confiscated by Simon:
"De' fuorusciti perseguia la ricchezze il nuovo Doge; e la mentita
Amelia alla rapace man sottrarle potea" (74–75; The new Doge
sought the wealth of the exiles; and the imposter Amelia was able to
save it from his rapacious grasp).

14. Both Amelia and her mother are named Maria.

15. Even Amelia's text emphasizes this divide, for while
Gutiérrez's Susana cries, " ¡Oh, padre!, ¡vivir escondida/ y solo para
ti!" (150; O father! I will live in concealment, live only for you),
Amelia is more restrained: "Padre! vedrai la vigile... figlia a te sempre
accanto" (93–94; Father! you will see your vigilant daughter always
near you).

16. The *Disposizione* notes that Simon, "almost startled, turns
around and answers PAOLO, 'Rinuncia ogni speranza.'" (Give up all
hope.) Busch II:444.

17. The Council scene is Boito's most visible contribution to the
revised libretto, tellingly juxtaposing the public and private sides of
Simon.

18. The staging of this moment further reinforces the symbolic
resonance of Simon's appeal, for the Doge steps toward the footlights

and practically out of the realistic stage scene: "At the words 'Piango su voi,' he takes a step forwards, and also at the words, 'E vo gridando: pace!'" Busch II:453.

19. Note the contrast in Paolo's own response here and in the final act, when Simon at last condemns him to death for participating in another rebellion: finding himself accursed, Paolo flees the Council chamber with a terrified "Orror" (150), while in the last act he announces his impending death to Fiesco with complete indifference (207).

20. In this scene, Verdi also establishes a musical connection highlighting the parallels between Simon and Gabriele. As Amelia prays to her mother in Heaven to intercede for Gabriele, the man whose faults stem "solo per troppo amor" (192; only from too much love), the vocal line foreshadows the motif of peace taken up by Simon when he at last achieves forgiveness from Fiesco for his own crimes, crimes flowing not from evil but from loving too much: "vien,.. ch'io ti stringa al petto, o... padre di Maria" (226–27; come, let me clasp you to my heart, father of Maria).

21. In this context, even the execution of Paolo, an afterthought by Boito, is stripped of any sense of personal vindictiveness; after the endless misery Paolo has inflicted on his fellow human beings, his death seems the triumphant expulsion of Evil itself.

22. The injustice of Fiesco's blind fury is made only too clear by his allusion to the torches that Simon has already ordered extinguished as a sign of respect for the dead.

23. Since Fiesco has been in hiding under the alias Andrea, Simon has, until now, been unable to return the old man's lost granddaughter to him and thus gain his forgiveness.

24. The *Disposizione* indicates, "towards the last bars of the duet, the DOGE and FIESCO embrace." Busch II:476.

25. Significantly, Simon has called her by this name only once before, when he first discovers her identity in Act I. In Gutiérrez's play, Simon dies not with this name on his lips, but with the more earth-bound address to Fiesco, "Vos..., Jacobo..., id,/ y mi voluntad... cumplid.../ Decidles... que es... mi deseo" (193; You, Jacobo, carry out my wish, the choice that I desire).

26. The stage directions in the *Disposizione* read, "suddenly the DOGE rises, extends his arms towards his daughter, and with a

supreme effort exclaims 'Maria!...' He would like to say more, but he cannot; he falls on to the chair, turns his eyes one last time towards the sea, his head falls backwards; he is dead." Busch II:479.

Otello

1. Letter to Florimo, 4 January 1871, in *I Copialettere,* 233. Translation in Budden, *The Operas of Verdi* III:266.

2. For further discussion of the musical innovations in the opera, see also Hepokoski, *Giuseppe Verdi: Otello.*

3. See also Styan, *Shakespeare's Stagecraft.*

4. Letter from Verdi to Morelli, 7 February 1880, in *I Copialettere,* 694.

5. Ricordi, *Disposizione,* 5.

6. *Othello the Moor of Venice,* in *The Riverside Shakespeare,* I.i.88–89. Hereafter, line numbers are cited in parentheses after the quotation.

7. *Macbeth,* in *The Riverside Shakespeare,* I.v.65–66.

8. *Otello,* 34. Hereafter, page numbers are cited in parentheses after the quotation.

9. Ricordi, *Disposizione,* 16.

10. Letter to Morelli, 24 September 1881, in Abbiati IV:184.

11. For more on Jago's game-playing, see also Pierre-Jean Rémy, "Otello et Othello," *L'Avant-Scène* 3 (1976):7–10.

12. Ricordi, *Disposizione,* 21.

13. The critic Filippo Filippi, reviewing the première of *Otello* for *La perseveranza,* wrote, "There is a descending chromatic scale for the baritone from F to G-sharp which is outright sinister and fatal." Busch II:683.

14. For further discussion of Verdi's insistence that Jago be deleted from the love scene, see also Martin, 527.

15. Letter to Boito, 3 May 1884, in *Carteggio Verdi-Boito,* 76.

16. For another view of the *Credo,* see also Schmidgall, "Incredible Credo?" in *Shakespeare and Opera,* 240–50.

17. Ricordi, *Disposizione,* 37.

18. See also Hepokoski, 146–47.

19. Ricordi, *Disposizione,* 37.

20. Ibid., 39.

21. Jago has already moved downstage to include the spectators in his prayer, "Or qui si tragga Otello!.. aiuta, aiuta, sàtana il mio cimento" (121; Now draw Otello here... help, Satan, help my venture). And his prayer seems to be answered: while in Shakespeare's play, Iago must bring Othello upon the scene himself, the opera suggests a darker undercurrent of Satanic influence with Otello's sudden arrival.

22. Ricordi, *Disposizione,* 39–40.

23. Ibid., 48.

24. Ibid., 54.

25. Letter to Verdi, 24 August 1881, in *Carteggio Verdi-Boito,* 58.

26. See also Verdi's letter to Boito, 15 August 1880, and Boito's letter, 18 October 1880, ibid., 1–6.

27. Letter to Ricordi, 9 February 1889, in Abbiati IV:372.

28. Ricordi, *Disposizione,* 80.

29. Regarding the staging of this final moment, Verdi's instincts proved more incisive than Boito's. As Victor Maurel, the first Jago, wrote, "The authors had contrary opinions on this subject; the poet thought and firmly believed that an ample gesture of contempt would suffice, with a body position and a facial expression befitting the situation. The musician, however, thought that Jago, by placing his heel on Otello's body lying unconscious at his feet, would make a much stronger impression and be in more accord with the Jago of the opera, who differs on several points from the Iago of Shakespeare's tragedy. To satisfy the poet fully, we followed his instructions on the night of the première; but on the succeeding nights we tried out the second version which conforms more to our feeling," *Otello Production Book by Victor Maurel,* Busch II:664.

30. Knight, *The Wheel of Fire,* 119.